# *Smoking*
# **Cessation**

### Editor: Katharine J. Palmer

**Adis International**

Auckland • Buenos Aires • Chester • Hong Kong • Madrid • Milan • Osaka • Paris • Philadelphia • São Paulo • Sydney

# Smoking Cessation

### Editor: Katharine J. Palmer

*A Wolters Kluwer Company*

**Commercial Manager: Gordon Mallarkey**
**Publication Manager: Lorna Venter-Lewis**
Adis International Limited
Copyright © 2000 Adis International Limited ISBN 0-86471-086-0

Earlier versions of some articles in this book were published in Adis International's peer-reviewed medical journals. The editor has collated the articles and worked with the authors to adapt and update the information for this publication.

Although great care has been taken in compiling and checking the information in this book to ensure it is accurate, the authors, the publisher and their servants or agents shall not be held responsible for the continued currency of the information or from any errors, omissions or inaccuracies arising therefrom, whether arising from negligence or otherwise howsoever or for any consequences arising therefrom.

Printed in Hong Kong.

# Foreword

Mark Twain said, 'I know I can quit smoking because I've done it a thousand times'. This humorous remark conveys the struggle that many smokers go through in attempting to break their addiction to nicotine. So, how can medicine help individuals who want to quit smoking?

Practical guidelines on the optimum use of the nicotine patch, gum, spray and inhaler are presented in this book, as are those for non-nicotine drug treatments. There are focussed articles on smoking cessation in the elderly and in patients with depression and coronary heart disease. Costs benefits are also highlighted.

This is an ideal book for healthcare professionals who want to give their patients the best chance to stop smoking.

*Katharine J. Palmer*
Editor, *CNS Drugs*

August 2000

CNS Drugs *is a highly-regarded international medical journal. The journal promotes rational pharmacotherapy and disease management within the disciplines of clinical psychiatry and neurology by publishing a regular programme of review articles in the subject area.*

# Smoking Cessation

# Contents

# Achieving Smoking Cessation in Nicotine-Dependent Individuals
## Practical Guidelines

*Michelle M. Mielke, Douglas E. Jorenby* and *Michael C. Fiore*

Center for Tobacco Research and Intervention, Division of General Internal Medicine, Department of Medicine, University of Wisconsin Medical School, Madison, Wisconsin, USA

Cigarette smoking is the single greatest preventable cause of illness and premature death in our society,[1] being responsible for more than 3 million deaths worldwide each year.[2] Despite awareness of this serious health threat and the availability of effective smoking cessation interventions, healthcare clinicians often fail to provide smoking cessation therapy to nicotine-dependent smokers.

Authoritative clinical practice guidelines are one method of reducing existing barriers that interfere with clinician-directed smoking cessation interventions. The US Agency for Health Care Policy and Research (AHCPR), part of the US Department of Health and Human Services, convened a panel of experts in 1994 to develop standard practice guidelines on the treatment of nicotine dependence and tobacco addiction. In April 1996, the AHCPR released the result of its 2-year, science-based review of the extant English-language smoking cessation literature. This resource, the AHCPR Smoking Cessation Clinical Practice Guideline,[3] provides evidence-based recommendations for primary care clinicians and smoking cessation specialists, as well as healthcare administrators, insurers and purchasers. Healthcare practitioners can promote smoking cessation in nicotine-dependent individuals by using this summary of the AHCPR recommendations.

## 1. Nicotine Replacement Therapy

Long term nicotine use usually leads to tolerance and physical dependence. Abrupt cessation of nicotine use in physically dependent smokers results in withdrawal symptoms such as anxiety, irritability, insomnia, difficulty concentrating and bodyweight gain.[4] Nicotine replacement therapy reduces some of the withdrawal symptoms associated with quitting smoking, and has been shown to be efficacious in increasing rates of smoking cessation, although the relationship between cessation efficacy and withdrawal symptom relief is variable.[3,5] All patients should be encouraged to use nicotine replacement therapy as an aid for smoking cessation, except in the presence of specific medical contraindications.[3] Controlled clinical trials have been published involving 4 different delivery forms of nicotine replacement therapy: the transdermal patch, polacrilex chewing gum, nasal spray and inhaler.[6]

**Table I.** Suggestions for the clinical use of the transdermal nicotine patch as an aid to smoking cessation[3]

| Parameter | Recommendations |
|---|---|
| Patient selection | Appropriate as a primary pharmacotherapy for smoking cessation |
| Precautions | *Pregnancy:* Pregnant smokers should first be encouraged to attempt cessation without pharmacological treatment. The nicotine patch should be used during pregnancy only if the increased likelihood of smoking cessation, with its potential benefits, outweighs the risk of nicotine replacement and potential concomitant smoking. Similar factors should be considered in lactating women |
| | *Cardiovascular diseases:* Although not an independent risk factor for acute myocardial events, the nicotine patch should be used only after consideration of risks and benefits among particular cardiovascular patient groups [e.g. those in the immediate (within 4 weeks) post-myocardial infarction period, those with serious arrhythmias and those with serious or worsening angina pectoris] |
| | *Skin reactions:* Up to 50% of patients using the nicotine patch will have a local skin reaction.[6] Skin reactions are usually mild and self-limiting, but may worsen over the course of therapy. Local treatment with hydrocortisone cream or triamcinolone cream (0.5%) and rotating sites of application may ameliorate such local reactions. In less than 5% of patients do such reactions require the discontinuation of nicotine patch treatment[6] |
| Dosage[a] | Treatment of 8 weeks or less has been shown to be as efficacious as longer treatment periods. Based on this finding, the following treatment schedules are suggested as reasonable for most smokers[b]: 4 weeks of full strength patch (15 mg/16h, 21 mg/24h or 22 mg/24h), then 2 to 4 weeks of lower strength patches |
| Prescribing instructions | *Abstinence from smoking:* The patient should refrain from smoking while using the patch |
| | *Location:* At the start of each day, the patient should place a new patch on a relatively hairless location between the neck and waist |
| | *Activities:* There are no restrictions while using the patch |
| | *Time:* Patches should be applied as soon as patients awaken on their quit day |

a   These dosage recommendations are based on a review of the published research literature and do not necessarily conform to package insert information.

b   Clinicians should consult the package insert for other treatment suggestions, including treatment without tapering, and should consider individualising treatment based on specific patient characteristics such as previous experience with the patch, number of cigarettes smoked, and degree of addiction.

## 1.1 Transdermal Nicotine Patch

A number of meta-analyses of the efficacy of the transdermal nicotine patch, summarising dozens of clinical trials, have been published.[7-11] The conclusion of independent meta-analyses is that use of the transdermal nicotine patch as a primary pharmacotherapy for smoking cessation approximately doubles 6- to 12-month abstinence rates over those produced by placebo, and that this effect is robust across a variety of adjuvant psychosocial intervention intensities.[3]

Clinical guidelines and treatment protocols regarding the use of the transdermal nicotine patch are highlighted in table I. Dosage recommendations are based on a review of the published research literature and do not necessarily conform to product insert recommendations.

The transdermal nicotine patch was approved by the US Food and Drug Administration (FDA) for over-the-counter (OTC) use in the US in April 1996; patches are also available OTC in other countries. Although the safety and efficacy of the nicotine patch are well established, nonprescription use of the patch is not without controversy. One study examining the effectiveness of nicotine patch use suggests that abstinence rates are lower when the nicotine patch is used without physician advice and assistance.[12] The potential absence of clinician counselling associated with nonprescription nicotine patch use may lead to lower abstinence rates, and may discourage patients from using nicotine patches during subsequent quit attempts. However, from a public health perspective, possible reductions in individual efficacy are likely to be offset by the increased access to nicotine patches that OTC availability offers. The net impact would be more successful cessation attempts overall.

Moreover, the nicotine patch is a highly effective aid to smoking cessation and is consistently more efficacious than placebo treatment regardless of the intensity of any adjuvant counselling.[3] However, intensive psychosocial interventions do increase the abstinence rates among nicotine patch users[3] and clinicians should, whenever possible, recommend and offer behavioural interventions. As a result, the recent AHCPR Guideline recommends the use of the nicotine patch in all patients attempting smoking cessation in the absence of medical contraindications.

### 1.2 Nicotine Polacrilex Gum

Of all the nicotine replacement therapies, nicotine polacrilex gum has the most extensive research and clinical history, having been available since the 1980s.[6] After over a decade of prescription use in the US, nicotine gum is now available for nonprescription use. It is currently available in many countries in two doses: 2mg or 4mg of nicotine per piece.

Numerous studies have demonstrated that nicotine gum improves smoking cessation rates over a 12-month period when compared with placebo.[3] Early meta-analyses concluded that nicotine gum was only effective when used in specialised smoking cessation clinics.[13] However, more recent meta-analyses, based on larger samples, have found that the efficacy of the gum is consistently greater than that of placebo, regardless of counselling intensity.[3] However, intensive psychosocial intervention adds to the effectiveness of nicotine gum, as is the case with transdermal nicotine.[3] Finally, data suggest that the 4mg nicotine gum dose is more effective than the 2mg dose in heavier smokers.[10]

Clinical guidelines and treatment protocols regarding the use of nicotine gum are highlighted in table II.

### 1.3 Nicotine Nasal Spray

Clinical recommendations regarding the use of nicotine nasal spray in smoking cessation were not included in the AHCPR Guideline. This was because the nasal spray had not been approved by the FDA at the time the Guideline was finalised, and because of the limited available literature on the efficacy of this method of replacement therapy.

However, several clinical trials now suggest significant benefit of the nasal spray compared with placebo interventions.[14-16] Two placebo-controlled studies found significantly higher 12-month abstinence rates with nicotine nasal spray in conjunction with group counselling than with placebo and counselling.[14,15] One placebo-controlled, double-blind trial concluded that nicotine nasal spray is well tolerated and efficacious in significantly increasing continuous abstinence over placebo for up to 1 year.[16] By allowing variable administration of nicotine on a short term basis, nicotine nasal spray may be useful in the treatment of highly dependent

**Table II.** Suggestions for the clinical use of nicotine chewing gum as an aid to smoking cessation[3]

| Parameter | Recommendations |
|---|---|
| Patient selection | Appropriate as a primary pharmacotherapy for smoking cessation |
| Precautions | *Pregnancy:* Pregnant smokers should first be encouraged to attempt cessation without pharmacological treatment. Nicotine gum should be used during pregnancy only if the increased likelihood of smoking cessation, with its potential benefits, outweighs the risk of nicotine replacement and potential concomitant smoking |
| | *Cardiovascular diseases:* Although not an independent risk factor for acute myocardial events, nicotine gum should be used only after consideration of risks and benefits among particular cardiovascular patient groups [e.g. those in the immediate (within 4 weeks) post-myocardial infarction period, those with serious arrhythmias and those with serious or worsening angina pectoris] |
| | *Adverse effects:* Common adverse effects of nicotine gum include mouth soreness, hiccups, dyspepsia and jaw ache.[6] These effects are generally mild and transient, and can often be alleviated by correcting the patient's chewing technique (see prescribing instructions below) |
| Dosage | Nicotine gum is available in doses of 2mg and 4mg per piece. Patients should be prescribed the 2mg gum initially. The 4mg gum should be prescribed to patients who express a preference for it, have failed to stop smoking with the 2mg gum but remain motivated to quit, and/or are highly dependent on nicotine. The gum is most commonly prescribed for the first few months of a quit attempt. Clinicians should tailor the duration of therapy to fit the needs of each patient. Patients using the 2mg strength should use not more than 30 pieces per day, whereas those using the 4mg strength should not exceed 20 pieces per day |
| Prescribing instructions | *Abstinence from smoking:* The patient should refrain from smoking while using the gum |
| | *Chewing technique:* The gum should be chewed slowly until a peppery taste emerges, then 'parked' between cheek and gum to facilitate nicotine absorption through the oral mucosa. Gum should be slowly and intermittently chewed and parked for about 30 minutes |
| | *Absorption:* Acidic beverages (e.g. coffee, juices, soft drinks) interfere with the buccal absorption of nicotine,[3] so eating and drinking anything except water should be avoided for 15 minutes before and during chewing the gum |
| | *Scheduling of dose:* A common problem is that patients do not use enough gum to get the maximum benefit; they chew too few pieces per day and do not use the gum for a sufficient number of weeks. Instructions to chew the gum on a fixed schedule (at least 1 piece every 1 to 2 hours) for at least 1 to 3 months may be more beneficial than *ad libitum* use |

smokers.[17] Indeed, one study demonstrated that nicotine nasal spray provided particular benefit to more heavily dependent smokers.[15]

Recommended administration regimens for the nicotine nasal spray are highlighted in table III.[17]

Despite moderate initial adverse effects,[14] promise for this relatively new form of nicotine replacement therapy exists based on its rapid rate of nicotine absorption[15] and ease of administration. Clinical studies are currently needed to compare the relative efficacy of transdermal nicotine, nicotine gum and nicotine nasal spray, alone and in combination with behavioural interventions.

### 1.4 Nicotine Inhaler

The nicotine inhaler was developed as an additional nicotine replacement delivery device. Although the inhaler resembles a cigarette, thus providing some oral and handling reinforcement, it does not deliver nicotine in the same manner as a cigarette, nor does it rely on combustion.[18] Instead, vaporised nicotine droplets are deposited in the oral and upper airway mucosa and absorbed transmucosally.[18]

The efficacy of the nicotine inhaler in promoting short term smoking cessation was demonstrated in three double-blind, placebo-controlled trials.[18,19,19a] One randomised, placebo-controlled trial of a nicotine inhaler demonstrated an increase in both short and long term abstinence rates when compared with a low intensity counselling intervention.[20] Abstinence rates may be enhanced even more if nicotine inhalers are used in combination with the patch and/or more intense behavioural interventions.[18-20]

At the time that the AHCPR Smoking Cessation Clinical Practice Guideline[3] was prepared, the nicotine inhaler was still an investigational drug. Therefore, no administration regimen is outlined.

## 1.5 Individualising Nicotine Replacement Therapy

All four types of nicotine replacement therapy (patch, gum, spray and inhaler) have been shown to be efficacious in smoking cessation treatment. However, the transdermal nicotine patch is preferable for routine clinical use because:[3]

- it is associated with fewer patient compliance problems;
- less clinician time is required to educate patients in its effective use;
- it is associated with fewer adverse effects.

**Table III.** Suggestions for the clinical use of nicotine nasal spray as an aid to smoking cessation[16]

| Parameter | Recommendation |
|---|---|
| Patient selection | Appropriate as adjunctive pharmacotherapy in the context of a comprehensive behavioural smoking cessation programme |
| Precautions | *Pregnancy:* Pregnant smokers should first be encouraged to attempt cessation without pharmacological treatment. Nicotine nasal spray should be used during pregnancy only if the increased likelihood of smoking cessation, with its potential benefits, outweighs the risk of nicotine replacement and potential concomitant smoking |
| | *Cardiovascular diseases:* Although not an independent risk factor for acute myocardial events, nicotine nasal spray should be used only after consideration of risks and benefits among particular cardiovascular patient groups [e.g. those in the immediate (within 4 weeks) post-myocardial infarction period, those with serious arrhythmias and those with serious or worsening angina pectoris] |
| | *Adverse effects:* Common adverse effects of nicotine nasal spray include nasal irritation, runny nose, throat irritation, watering eyes, sneezing and cough.[6] These effects are usually moderate or severe initially, but the frequency and severity of effects may decline with continued use[14] |
| Dosage | Nicotine nasal spray is available in a metered-dose inhaler. One dose equals 1mg of nicotine (2 × 0.5mg sprays, 1 in each nostril). Patients should be prescribed 1 to 2 doses per hour initially. Administration may be increased up to a maximum recommended dosage of 5mg (10 sprays) per hour or 40mg (80 sprays) per day. Recommended duration of use is up to 8 weeks, then use should be discontinued over the subsequent 4 to 6 weeks. Sustained use of nicotine nasal spray beyond 6 months is not recommended and should be discouraged |
| Prescribing instructions | *Abstinence from smoking:* The patient should refrain from smoking while using the nicotine nasal spray |
| | *Scheduling of dose:* Patients should use the recommended minimum of 8 doses per day, and should not exceed the recommended maximum dose per hour or per day (see above) |
| | *Discontinuation of use:* No tapering strategy has been shown to be optimal.[17] Patients may use only half a dose at a time, use the spray less frequently, set a planned 'quit date' for stopping use of the spray, or may simply stop using the spray |

Conversely, indications for use of nicotine gum include patient preference, previous failure with the nicotine patch, and contraindications specific to nicotine patch use such as adverse skin reactions.[3] Because of the more limited published literature on the nicotine inhaler and spray, specific indications and contraindications for these agents have not been clearly identified.

The utility of individualising nicotine replacement therapy to specific patient characteristics such as degree of physical dependence, previous experience with specific smoking cessation aids, etc., is an area of active interest and clinical research. Currently there is little consistent evidence that specialised assessments of patient characteristics, such as degree of nicotine dependence, psychiatric comorbidity or motivation for quitting, predict the efficacy of various interventions.[3] That is, smoking cessation treatment is effective without such specialised assessments.

Because heavier smokers (typically using more than 25 cigarettes per day) generally have less success in maintaining long term abstinence, a good deal of attention has focused on developing better treatments for this subpopulation. Since nicotine replacement therapies typically only replace a portion of the serum nicotine concentrations that are present during tobacco use, researchers and clinicians have hypothesised that heavy smokers in particular may be underdosed by standard treatment regimens. Evidence supporting this hypothesis has been observed by the superior response of heavy smokers to 4mg, compared with 2mg, nicotine gum.[21] With the fixed administration system of transdermal nicotine, however, a large study found no sustained differences in cessation rates between 22 and 44mg patch doses for either heavy or light smokers.[5]

Unless additional research indicates a positive association between precessation nicotine concentration and the percentage replacement level from nicotine patch use, there does not appear to be a clear indication to provide heavy smokers with higher doses of transdermal nicotine. There are consistent data, however, to recommend initiating therapy with the 4mg nicotine dose of gum in heavier smokers.

Most smokers should follow the transdermal nicotine treatment regimens outlined in table I. The limited research available on the use of transdermal nicotine with light smokers (patients who smoke 10 to 15 cigarettes per day) suggests that a lower initial dose (10 to 14mg) may be used.[3] Similarly, if nicotine gum is preferred, light smokers may begin with a 2mg dose (see table II). If the 2mg dose of gum has been unsuccessful in relieving withdrawal symptoms and craving in previous quit attempts, the 4mg dose may be substituted.

### 1.6 Combined Nicotine Replacement Therapies

Combination pharmacotherapy for smoking cessation holds much promise in increasing the absolute abstinence rates of the nicotine replacement therapies currently used individually. The addition of nicotine gum to nicotine patch use in individuals smoking more than 10 cigarettes per day increased short term abstinence rates in 1 placebo-controlled clinical trial.[22]

Possible beneficial effects of alternative combinations of nicotine replacement therapies (i.e. nicotine patch plus nicotine inhaler), and particular populations who would benefit from them, need to be elucidated through further study.

## 2. Other Pharmacotherapies

### 2.1 Amfebutamone (Bupropion) SR

Amfebutamone (bupropion) sustained-release (SR) is an atypical antidepressant with action on both dopaminergic and noradrenergic pathways in the brain and is the only non-nicotine therapy approved for a smoking cessation indication by the US FDA. One large multicentre study demonstrated that amfebutamone SR was superior to placebo in producing long term abstinence (23% *vs* 12% at 12 months, respectively), and that a dosage of 150mg twice daily produced the highest cessation rates.[20a] A larger study confirmed the superiority of amfebutamone SR over placebo (30.3% *vs* 15.6% at 12 months, respectively) and also tested whether a combination of amfebutamone SR and a nicotine patch treatment produced superior outcomes; cessation rates at 12 months were not statistically significant for the combination therapy (35.5%) versus bupropion SR alone (30.3%).[20b] The efficacy of amfebutamone SR when combined with *ad lib* nicotine replacement therapies is unknown at present. Amfebutamone SR was effective at reducing the severity of nicotine withdrawal symptoms, and also delayed post-cessation weight gain.[20b] At the time of the AHCPR Smoking Cessation Clinical Practice Guideline,[3] the use of amfebutamone in smoking cessation was currently under investigation. Now, recent studies suggest the use of amfebutamone as both a primary and adjunctive pharmacotherapy for achieving smoking cessation in nicotine dependent individuals.

### 2.2 Other Interventions

Several other pharmacological interventions investigated as smoking cessation aids, including clonidine, anxiolytics, mecamylamine and antidepressants, have met with varying degrees of success.

Clonidine, an $\alpha_2$-noradrenergic agonist, has been shown to reduce nicotine withdrawal symptoms in highly dependent cigarette smokers, and its usefulness as a pharmacotherapy for smoking cessation has been evaluated.[23] Meta-analytic reviews have concluded that there is little support for the use of clonidine either as a primary or adjunctive pharmacological treatment for smoking cessation.[3] One double-blind, randomised trial suggested that clonidine may be differentially effective in female patients,[23] but adverse effects are common, and as many as 25% of patients may discontinue clonidine therapy for this reason.[3]

Only a few trials have evaluated anxiolytics as a treatment for smoking cessation. One study using buspirone revealed evidence of efficacy in smoking cessation.[3] However, the AHCPR Guideline reached no conclusions regarding the efficacy of anxiolytics in smoking cessation because of the paucity of clinical research data.[3]

One randomised, double-blind, placebo-controlled trial demonstrated increased abstinence rates with mecamylamine, a nicotine antagonist, plus nicotine patch therapy versus placebo plus nicotine patch.[24]

Smoking is significantly more prevalent among individuals with a history of depression, and these individuals have more difficulty quitting smoking than do smokers without such a history.[25-27] A history of major depression was also associated with more severe nicotine withdrawal in a large epidemiological study.[26] Antidepressants have therefore been proposed as potential aids in smoking cessation, but additional research regarding the efficacy of antidepressants, with the exception of amfebutamone, in smoking cessation therapy is needed

**Table IV.** Common elements of problem-solving/skills-training smoking cessation counselling[3]

| Problem-solving treatment component | Examples |
|---|---|
| *Recognition of danger situations:* Identification of events, internal states or activities that are thought to increase the risk of smoking or relapse | Being around other smokers |
| | Being under time pressure |
| | Getting into an argument |
| | Experiencing urges or negative moods |
| | Drinking alcohol |
| *Coping skills:* Identification and practice of coping or problem-solving skills. Typically, these skills are intended to cope with danger situations (see above) | Learning to anticipate and avoid danger situations |
| | Learning cognitive strategies that will reduce negative moods |
| | Accomplishing lifestyle changes that reduce stress, improve quality of life or produce pleasure |
| | Learning cognitive and behavioural activities that distract attention from smoking urges |
| *Basic information:* Provision of basic information about smoking and successful quitting | The nature/time course of withdrawal |
| | The addictive nature of smoking |
| | The fact that any smoking (even a single puff) increases the likelihood of full relapse |

**Table V.** Common elements of supportive smoking cessation counselling[3]

| Supportive treatment component | Examples |
|---|---|
| Encourage the patient in the quit attempt | Note that effective cessation treatments are now available |
| | Note that half of all people who have ever smoked have now quit |
| | Communicate belief in patient's ability to quit |
| Communicate caring and concern | Ask how the patient feels about quitting |
| | Directly express concern and willingness to help |
| | Be open to the patient's expression of fears of quitting, difficulties experienced and ambivalent feelings |
| Encourage the patient to talk about the quitting process | Ask about: |
| | reasons the patient wants to quit |
| | difficulties encountered while quitting |
| | success the patient has achieved |
| | concerns or worries about quitting |
| Provide basic information about smoking and successful quitting | The nature/time course of withdrawal |
| | The addictive nature of smoking |
| | The fact that any smoking (even a single puff) increases the likelihood of full relapse |

before firm conclusions can be drawn. Research on such agents is ongoing and these results should clarify the potential role of antidepressant agents in treating tobacco addiction.

## 3. Behavioural Therapy

According to the meta-analyses conducted by the AHCPR expert panel, behavioural smoking cessation interventions delivered by a wide variety of healthcare professionals (physicians, nurses, pharmacists, psychologists, dentists, etc.) increase cessation rates relative to self-help interventions.[3] Based on the strength of this finding, the panel recommended that all clinicians routinely deliver smoking cessation messages at every clinical contact with their patients who smoke. Of particular interest were a number of studies that utilised multiple provider interventions; patients receiving cessation messages from different members of the healthcare team (their physician, nurse, psychologist, etc.) were 3 times more likely to quit than those receiving no message.[3] Thus, there appears to be a synergistic effect of involving the entire healthcare team in smoking cessation interventions.

The AHCPR Guideline examined three basic types of behavioural intervention: (i) self-help; (ii) individual counselling; and (iii) group counselling. While self-help pamphlets and patient education materials are some of the most ubiquitous smoking cessation aids, meta-analyses suggested that, when used alone, they were not significantly more effective in promoting cessation than no intervention.[3] Both individual and group counselling were found to increase cessation rates relative to no intervention.[3] The meta-analytic process also identified specific counselling components that were effective in promoting smoking cessation: general problem-solving/skills-training (e.g. identifying situations with a high risk of relapse, practising coping skills; see table IV) and clinician-provided social support (e.g. encouragement, caring, active listening to patient concerns; see table V).[3]

It is recommended that all smokers willing to enter an intensive smoking cessation programme be encouraged to participate, as the AHCPR Guideline found a clear positive dose-response relationship between both intensity and frequency of counselling and long term cessation.[3] As delineated in the Guideline, an intensive smoking cessation programme would include either individual or group counselling of at least 4 to 7 sessions, each lasting 20 to 30 minutes, spanning at least 2 weeks and preferably more than 8 weeks.[3] However, it was also true that brief clinician advice (<3 minutes) reliably produced cessation rates superior to no intervention.[3] Given that many smokers opt not to participate in intensive cessation programmes,[28] the importance of offering brief advice at every clinical contact cannot be overemphasised.

## 4. Other Treatments

Finally, other nonpharmacological treatments such as hypnosis and acupuncture were evaluated by the AHCPR panel. In both cases, the empirical evidence was very limited, contradictory, and generally of poor quality. Because of this, the panel concluded that insufficient evidence exists to support the efficacy of either hypnosis or acupuncture as smoking cessation treatments.[3]

## 5. Conclusion

Based on a thorough review and analysis of the literature, it can be unequivocally stated that selective smoking cessation interventions are effective and should be provided to every person who uses tobacco. The recently released AHCPR Smoking Cessation Clinical Practice Guideline has identified three treatment elements that particularly enhance smoking cessation: (i) clinician-provided social support; (ii) problem-solving/skills-training; and (iii) nicotine replacement therapy. The universal application of these effective treatments hold great promise in reducing the greatest preventable cause of illness and death in our society, tobacco addiction.

### References

1. Centers for Disease Control. Reducing the health consequences of smoking: 25 years of progress – a report of the Surgeon General, 1989. Rockville (MD): U.S. Department of Health and Human Services, Public Health Service, 1989. DHHS publication No. (CDC) 89-8411
2. Peto R, Lopez AD, Boreham J, et al. Mortality from smoking worldwide. Br Med Bull 1996; 52: 12-21
3. Fiore MC, Bailey WC, Cohen SJ, et al. Smoking cessation. Clinical Practice Guideline No. 18. Rockville (MD): U.S. Department of Health and Human Services, Public Health Service, Agency for Health Care Policy and Research, 1996. AHCPR Publication No. 96-0692
4. American Psychiatric Association. Diagnostic and statistical manual of mental disorders. 4th ed. Washington, DC: American Psychiatric Association, 1994
5. Jorenby DE, Smith SS, Fiore MC, et al. Varying nicotine patch dose and type of smoking cessation counseling. JAMA 1995; 274: 1347-52

6.   Jorenby DE, Keehn DS, Fiore MC. Comparative efficacy and tolerability of nicotine replacement therapies. CNS Drugs 1995; 3: 227-36
7.   Fiore MC, Smith SS, Jorenby DE, et al. The effectiveness of the nicotine patch for smoking cessation: a meta-analysis. JAMA 1994; 271: 1940-7
8.   Gourlay S. The pros and cons of transdermal nicotine therapy. Med J Aust 1994; 160: 152-9
9.   Po ALW. Transdermal nicotine in smoking cessation: a meta-analysis. Eur J Clin Pharmacol 1993; 45: 519-28
10.  Silagy C, Mant D, Fowler G, et al. Meta-analysis on efficacy of nicotine replacement therapies in smoking cessation. Lancet 1994; 343: 139-42
11.  Tang JL, Law M, Wald N. How effective is nicotine replacement therapy in helping people to stop smoking? BMJ 1994; 308: 21-6
12.  Pierce JP, Gilpin E, Farkas AJ. Nicotine patch use in the general population: results from the 1993 California tobacco survey. J Natl Cancer Inst 1995; 87: 87-93
13.  Lam W, Sze PC, Sacks HS, et al. Meta-analysis of randomised controlled trials of nicotine chewing gum. Lancet 1987; 2: 27-30
14.  Hjalmarson A, Franzon M, Westin A, et al. Effect of nicotine nasal spray on smoking cessation: a randomized, placebo-controlled, double-blind study. Arch Intern Med 1994; 154: 2567-72
15.  Sutherland G, Stapleton JA, Russell MAH, et al. Randomised controlled trial of nasal nicotine spray in smoking cessation. Lancet 1992; 340: 324-9
16.  Schneider NG, Olmstead R, Mody FV, et al. Efficacy of a nicotine nasal spray in smoking cessation: a placebo-controlled, double-blind trial. Addiction 1995; 90: 1671-82
17.  McNeil Consumer Products Co. Nicotrol NS (nicotine nasal spray) package insert. Fort Washington (PA): McNeil Consumer Products Co., 1996
18.  Schneider NG, Olmstead R, Nilsson F, et al. Efficacy of a nicotine inhaler in smoking cessation: a double-blind, placebo-controlled trial. Addiction 1996; 91: 1293-306
19.  Leischow SJ, Nilsson F, Franzon M, et al. Efficacy of the nicotine inhaler as an adjunct to smoking cessation. Am J Health Behav 1996; 20: 364-71
19a. Hjalmarson A, Nilsson F, Sjostrom L, et al. The nicotine inhaler in smoking cessation. Arch Intern Med 1997; 157: 1721-8
20.  Tonnesen P, Norregaard J, Mikkelsen K, et al. A double-blind trial of a nicotine inhaler for smoking cessation. JAMA 1993; 269: 1268-71
20a. Hurt RD, Sachs DPL, Glover ED, et al. A comparison of sustained-release bupropion and placebo for smoking cessation. N Engl J Med 1997; 337: 1195-202
20b. Jorenby DE, Leischow SJ, Nides MA, et al. A controlled trial of sustained-release bupropion, a nicotine patch, or both for smoking cessation. N Engl J Med 1999; 340: 685-91
21.  Sachs DPL. Effectiveness of the 4mg dose of nicotine polacrilex for the initial treatment of high-dependent smokers. Arch Intern Med 1995; 155: 1973-80
22.  Kornitzer M, Boutsen M, Dramaix M, et al. Combined use of nicotine patch and gum in smoking cessation: a placebo-controlled clinical trial. Prev Med 1995; 24: 41-7
23.  Glassman AH, Stetner F, Walsh BT, et al. Heavy smokers, smoking cessation, and clonidine: results of a double-blind, randomized trial. JAMA 1988; 259: 2863-6
24.  Rose JE, Behm FM, Westman EC, et al. Mecamylamine combined with nicotine skin patch facilitates smoking cessation beyond nicotine patch treatment alone. Clin Pharmacol Ther 1994; 56: 86-99
25.  Anda RF, Williamson DF, Escobedo LG, et al. Depression and the dynamics of smoking: a national perspective. JAMA 1990; 264: 1541-5
26.  Breslau N, Kilbey MM, Andreski P. Nicotine withdrawal symptoms and psychiatric disorders: findings from an epidemiologic study of young adults. Am J Psychiatry 1992; 149: 464-9
27.  Glassman AH, Helzer JE, Covey LS, et al. Smoking, smoking cessation, and major depression. JAMA 1990; 264: 1546-9
28.  Lichtenstein E, Hollis J. Patient referral to a smoking cessation program: who follows through? J Fam Pract 1992; 34: 739-44

Correspondence: Dr *Douglas E. Jorenby,* Center for Tobacco Research and Intervention, 1930 Monroe Street, Suite 200, Madison, WI 53711, USA.
Email: dej@ctri.medicine.wisc.edu

# Non-Nicotine Pharmacotherapy for Smoking Cessation
## Mechanisms and Prospects

*Neal L. Benowitz* and *Margaret Wilson Peng*

Clinical Pharmacology Unit of the Medical Service, San Francisco General Hospital
Medical Center and the Departments of Medicine, Psychiatry and Biopharmaceutical
Sciences, University of California, San Francisco, California, USA

## 1. Do We Need Non-Nicotine Therapies to Aid Smoking Cessation?

Nicotine replacement therapy (NRT) has been the mainstay of smoking cessation therapy.[1] All of the nicotine products that have been marketed to date, including nicotine polacrilex gum, transdermal nicotine, nicotine nasal spray and the nicotine inhaler, enhance quitting about two-fold compared with placebo.[1-4] The absolute quit rates depend on the intensity of concomitant behavioural therapy, ranging from 10 to 30% at 1 year in controlled clinical trials.

The question remains – why do 70 to 90% of smokers fail to quit despite NRT? Undoubtedly, there are a variety of explanations, ranging from not being psychologically ready to quit to failure to respond to the medication. A discussion of psychological readiness is beyond the scope of this review. Failure to respond to nicotine medications should not be surprising. Smokers smoke for different reasons and respond differently to smoking cessation. Characteristics of smokers that might affect the response to nicotine therapy are summarised in table I. For example, in some individuals quit attempts are terminated because of mood disturbances, including profound depression.[5,6] In others, hunger and bodyweight gain prompt relapse. Still others experience cognitive impairment, stressful personal situations and/or alcohol or substance abuse which prompt relapse. Some people are afraid to use NRT for fear of continued exposure to an addictive drug, the fear of aggravating known heart disease or of causing problems during pregnancy. Symptoms of nicotine withdrawal are substantially relieved by NRT in some smokers but not in others. If the right medication could be matched with the right smoker, it is likely that smoking cessation would be facilitated in many or most smokers.

At present, a number of non-nicotine medications to aid smoking cessation are under development. Guidelines for selecting which medication is best for

**Table I.** Characteristics of smokers that may influence response to pharmacotherapy to aid smoking cessation

| |
|---|
| Age |
| Gender |
| Ethnicity |
| Level of dependence |
| Number and nature of prior quit attempts |
| Depression |
| Other psychiatric morbidity |
| Alcohol or substance abuse |
| Pregnancy |
| Medical illness (especially heart disease) |

which smokers are still lacking. This review will examine mechanisms and prospects for various non-nicotine medications.

## 2. Mechanisms of Nicotine Replacement Therapy

Before discussing mechanisms by which newer therapies work, it is useful to examine how nicotine is believed to work to aid smoking cessation. The original concept for NRT was to supply nicotine to prevent withdrawal symptoms that occur after smoking cessation.[7] Many clinical trials have confirmed that NRT does reduce withdrawal symptoms, although some symptoms are reduced only partially.[2,7,8] Hunger and bodyweight gain may be suppressed to some extent while using nicotine compared with placebo and the degree of suppression appears to be greater with higher doses of nicotine.[9,10] However, once nicotine is stopped, bodyweight increases to the same degree that occurs in the smoker who quits without nicotine.

Nicotine probably works by other mechanisms as well. Some smokers smoke to obtain perceived beneficial effects of nicotine, such as arousal, reduced fatigue or relaxation. It is not clear to what extent these are primary reinforcing effects of nicotine or whether these result from reversal of nicotine-induced withdrawal symptoms. Some NRTs, such as nicotine nasal spray, and to a lesser extent nicotine polacrilex gum and the nicotine inhaler, may produce some positive reinforcing effects, resembling those of a cigarette.

Another possible mechanism is that long term nicotine exposure, as occurs with regular tobacco use, is associated with desensitisation of some (but not all) subtypes of nicotinic cholinergic receptors.[11-13] For example, whereas in the sensitised state nicotine acting on noradrenergic neurons enhances noradrenaline (norepinephrine) release, in the desensitised (tolerant) state the release of noradrenaline would be blunted. Nicotine-induced desensitisation of nicotinic cholinergic receptors could result in a state in which noradrenaline release that would normally be stimulated by endogenous acetylcholine would be impaired.[12,14] The same phenomenon could occur for the effects of nicotine on other neurotransmitter systems.

In regular smokers, substantial levels of nicotine are maintained in the blood, and, therefore, the brain, for most of the day and even through the night. It is possible that for such smokers the state of having desensitised nicotine receptors is in itself rewarding. For example, noradrenaline release is associated with behavioural activation, as part of the stress-response system. Desensitisation of noradrenaline release could result in a calming effect, which is reported by some smokers.

NRTs with sustained release properties, such as transdermal nicotine, would also be expected to desensitise nicotine receptors, producing a desirable state in the abstinent smoker either by desensitisation *per se* and/or by blunting the reinforcing effects of any cigarette that might be smoked during a cessation slip. The latter idea is supported by observations that in abstinent smokers, smoking a cigarette is less rewarding when they are using nicotine patches.[15,16] Of note is the finding that low levels of nicotine, lower than those that activate nicotinic receptors, may desensitise those same nicotinic receptors.[17] This may explain the apparent benefit of nicotine gum or low dose nicotine patches despite resultant blood nicotine levels that are much lower than those achieved by cigarette smoking. As noted previously, some nicotinic receptor subtypes are desensitised more than others, suggesting that both nicotine agonism and desensitisation mechanisms could operate at the same time.

## 3. Nicotine Addiction and Mechanisms of Non-Nicotine Pharmacotherapies

### 3.1 Nicotine Addiction

A brief discussion of nicotine addiction provides a foundation for understanding various pharmacotherapies to aid smoking cessation.

The action of nicotine on nicotinic cholinergic receptors in the brain is primarily to enhance the release of various neurotransmitters.[18] These neurotransmitters include dopamine, noradrenaline, acetylcholine, serotonin (5-hydroxytryptamine; 5-HT), vasopressin, β-endorphin, glutamate, γ-aminobutyric acid (GABA) and others. There are various subtypes of nicotinic cholinergic receptors, and they are located in different parts of the brain.[19] The relationship between specific receptor subtypes and the release of specific neurotransmitters has not been fully elucidated. The release of neurotransmitters is believed to mediate psychological effects such as arousal, relaxation, cognitive enhancement, relief of stress and depression, etc. As described in section 2, prolonged exposure to nicotine desensitises many nicotinic cholinergic receptors, which results in a state in which the presence of nicotine is needed just to maintain normal neurotransmission. Stopping smoking results in subnormal neurotransmitter release, and individuals experience a state of neurotransmitter deficiency resulting in lethargy, irritability, restlessness, inability to concentrate, depression, etc.

The actions of nicotine on dopaminergic and noradrenergic systems in the brain seem to be particularly important in reinforcing nicotine self-administration. The mesolimbic dopamine system, ascending from the ventral tegmental area in the midbrain to the nucleus accumbens, olfactory tubercles and amygdala, is believed to mediate or signal pleasure and other critical rewards from nicotine, as well as rewards from other drugs of abuse including cocaine, heroin (diamorphine) and alcohol.[20-22]

The noradrenergic system includes the locus ceruleus, the largest noradrenergic nucleus in the brain. Activation of the locus ceruleus produces behavioural arousal and is a component of the body's defence reaction to stressful situations. Acutely, nicotine increases burst firing of the locus ceruleus.[23] Nicotine also activates the hypothalamic-pituitary system, causing the release of corticotropin (adrenocorticotropic hormone; ACTH) and cortisol via the noradrenergic system.[24]

The release of serotonin has been suggested to be involved in the modulation of mood and appetite. Nicotine treatment may increase or decrease brain serotonin levels in animals.[25,26] The role of serotonin release as a reward mechanism for nicotine dependence is suggested by rat studies in which the reinforcing effects of nicotine were reduced by selective serotonin (5-HT$_3$) antagonists.[27]

**Table II.** Mechanisms of pharmacotherapy of smoking cessation

**Nicotinic cholinergic receptor agonism**
Nicotine
Lobeline
Novel nicotine analogues

**Nicotine-like effects**
Antidepressants
  amfebutamone (bupropion)
  nortriptyline, doxepin
  fluoxetine
  moclobemide
Clonidine

**Nicotinic cholinergic receptor antagonism**
Mecamylamine

**Sensory stimulation/aversion**
Citric/ascorbic acid inhalers or spray
Silver acetate

**Others**
Buspirone
Corticotropin (adrenocorticotropic hormone; ACTH)

### 3.2 General Mechanisms of Non-Nicotine Therapies

The general mechanisms of action of non-nicotine therapies to aid smoking cessation are summarised in table II. It is important to note that these mechanisms are hypothetical, based on current concepts of the pharmacology of the drugs and of the nicotine addiction process.

One mechanism is simulation of the effect of nicotine. Drugs that mimic the neurochemical effects of nicotine, such as by increasing brain levels of dopamine, noradrenaline and/or serotonin, are expected to counteract the neurochemical deficiency state produced by nicotine withdrawal (fig. 1). Drugs may also simulate the actions of nicotine on brain reward systems. For example, the release of noradrenaline via stimulation of the locus ceruleus is believed to be involved in nicotine reward. At the same time, however, some drugs that reduce the firing of the locus ceruleus, such as amfebutamone (bupropion) and clonidine (see sections 4.1.1 and 4.2), appear to have benefit in smoking cessation. The benefit of inhibiting locus ceruleus firing might occur because it resembles the desensitised state seen with continuous nicotine stimulation and/or because it blocks pathways of acute nicotine stimulation.

Another general mechanism is nicotinic receptor antagonism. For example, mecamylamine blocks the rewarding effects of nicotine, acting noncompetitively on nicotinic receptor ion channels.[28,29] Mecamylamine administration alone increases cigarette smoking at least in the short term, presumably because the smoker is attempting to overcome the blockade.[30,31] How-

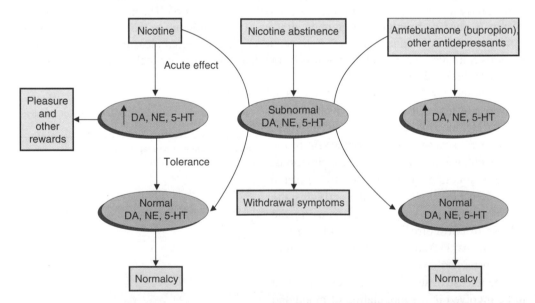

**Fig. 1.** Nicotine simulation hypothesis for the mechanism of action of non-nicotine medications for smoking cessation. *Left Panel:* Nicotine acutely releases neurotransmitters, including dopamine (DA), noradrenaline (norepinephrine; NA) and serotonin (5-hydroxytryptamine; 5-HT), which produce pleasure and other rewards. With prolonged exposure to nicotine, tolerance develops to these effects, and the presence of nicotine in the brain becomes necessary to maintain normal function.
*Centre Panel:* After quitting smoking, a state of nicotine abstinence ensues, resulting in subnormal levels of dopamine, noradrenaline and serotonin in the brain with associated withdrawal symptoms.
*Right Panel:* Amfebutamone (bupropion) and other antidepressants release and/or inhibit the reuptake of dopamine, noradrenaline and serotonin, thereby increasing levels of these neurotransmitters and simulating the actions of nicotine, and producing a state of normal mental functioning.

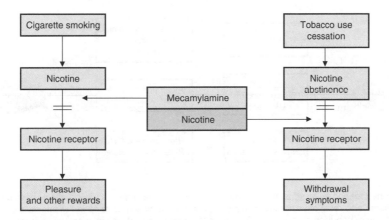

**Fig. 2.** Mecamylamine plus nicotine for smoking cessation. Mecamylamine antagonises the actions of nicotine on nicotinic cholinergic receptors, diminishing the reinforcing effects of nicotine delivered from cigarette smoke. Nicotine is coadministered, providing enough nicotinic cholinergic stimulation to blunt nicotine withdrawal symptoms and to counteract the potential toxic cardiovascular effects of mecamylamine.

ever, mecamylamine combined with nicotine appears to block the reinforcing effects of smoking while at the same time providing enough nicotine receptor stimulation to reduce withdrawal symptoms and to counteract the potential adverse effects of mecamylamine on the autonomic nervous system (fig. 2; section 4.4).[32]

Recently, there have been reports that amfebutamone, as well as some other antidepressants, are functional antagonists of nicotinic cholinergic receptors in muscle and autonomic ganglia.[33,34] These drugs do not block nicotine binding to receptors, but reduce the response of receptors to stimulation by nicotine. Whether antidepressants antagonise brain nicotine receptors and, if so, whether or not these drugs are present in high enough concentrations in the brain to significantly affect nicotine receptor function, remains to be determined.

### 3.3 Conditioned Responses

Nicotine is an essential factor in tobacco addiction.[18,35] People do not smoke cigarettes that do not contain nicotine, and most people do not smoke cigarettes with very low nicotine yields. When nicotine is delivered by cigarette smoking, it is associated with a complex experience of smells, tastes and sensory effects in the upper airway and lungs. Over time, the experience of smoking a cigarette becomes associated with the nicotine-mediated reward. Thus, as a consequence of conditioning, the smell, taste and feel of cigarette smoking become enjoyable (rewarding) [fig. 3]. After brief abstinence from regular cigarette smoking, either smoking a cigarette that does not contain nicotine or stimulating the throat with nicotine sensory substitutes such as citric acid have been shown to reduce withdrawal symptoms and craving (see section 4.5).[36-38] While these approaches alone have not shown promise in promoting long term cessation, sensory stimulants might enhance the efficacy of nicotine medications or other medications.

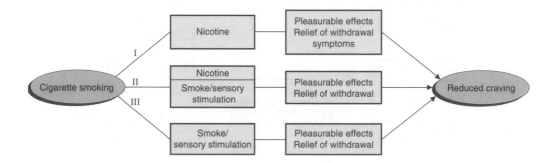

**Fig. 3.** Conditioned responses to sensory stimulation. Initially, cigarette smoking, via the effects of nicotine, produces pleasurable effects and relief of withdrawal symptoms, the latter of which develop in the interval between smoking cigarettes (I). In time, conditioning occurs such that the taste and smell of cigarette smoke become associated with the pharmacological activity of nicotine (II). After smoking cessation, the taste and smell of cigarette smoke, even in the absence of nicotine, can reproduce some of the reinforcing effects of smoking nicotine-containing cigarettes (III). However, this conditioned sensory reward is likely to be short-lived as deconditioning occurs in the absence of concomitant nicotine administration.

Related to sensory conditions in smoking are the aversive therapies such as silver acetate (see section 4.6). The silver combines with tobacco smoke to form bad tasting salts, which discourage smoking.

## 4. Specific Non-Nicotinic Therapies

This review is focused primarily on drugs for which we have located controlled clinical trial data for smoking cessation. Some therapies without controlled clinical trial data but which are of interest because of novelty or for historical reasons will also be mentioned.

### 4.1 Antidepressants

As a class, antidepressants are the most common non-nicotine drugs to have been shown to be of benefit in smoking cessation. A link between smoking and depression has been clearly demonstrated. Smokers are more likely than nonsmokers to have symptoms of depression.[39] Smokers with a history of depression are also likely to be more dependent on nicotine and have a lower likelihood of successfully quitting.[40,41] When they do quit, depression is more apt to be a prominent withdrawal symptom.[42] Cases of psychotic depression after smoking cessation have been reported.[5]

Although the association between smoking and depression is well established, the mechanism of benefit of antidepressant drugs to aid smoking cessation has not been determined. One hypothesis is that the neurochemical effects of nicotine, including the release of noradrenaline, dopamine and serotonin in the brain, are similar to the effects of antidepressants, as discussed in section 2 (fig. 1). Cigarette smoking, through a mechanism other than nicotine, is also associated with a reduction of brain monoamine oxidase (MAO)-A and -B activity, an effect that could have some antidepressant consequences.[43,44] Alternatively, it has been hypothesised that both depression and cigarette smoking reflect a common genetic predisposition, as is the case for the association between nicotine and alcohol abuse.[45]

### 4.1.1 Amfebutamone (Bupropion)

At present, amfebutamone is the only non-nicotine drug approved by the US Food and Drug Administration (FDA) for smoking cessation (it is also registered for use in this indication in the EU).

Amfebutamone is an aminoketone, structurally related to phenethylamines and resembling the anorectic drug diethylpropion. It is believed to aid smoking cessation by blocking the neuronal reuptake of dopamine and noradrenaline, and possibly by decreasing firing of the locus ceruleus.[46,47] As noted in section 3.2, amfebutamone may also functionally antagonise some nicotinic cholinergic receptors.[33] It has stimulant properties that may counteract the lethargy often associated with nicotine withdrawal. A significant portion of the activity of amfebutamone appears to be mediated by active metabolites, including hydroxy-amfebutamone.[47]

Amfebutamone is marketed for smoking cessation in a sustained release formulation. For depression, it is available in both immediate release and sustained release forms. The sustained release preparation results in slower absorption with less intense acute psychoactive effects following individual doses, allows for less frequent dose administration, and may be safer with respect to seizure risk compared with the immediate release preparation.

Two large clinical trials and a number of smaller ones have shown that amfebutamone facilitates smoking cessation.[48-51] In the trial by Hurt et al.[48] the drug was started 7 days prior to the quit date, allowing time for accumulation of amfebutamone and its metabolites to steady-state concentrations.[48] A sustained release formulation was given in two divided doses daily and was continued for 6 weeks after the quit date. The 615 smokers, who were screened not to have current depression, showed a dose response for cessation rates over the dosage range of 100, 150 or 300 mg/day. At the end of treatment, the point prevalence rate of smoking cessation was 44.2% among individuals who received 300 mg/ day versus 19.0% among those who received placebo. The respective point prevalence cessation rates at 1 year were 23.1 and 12.4%.

The trial by Jorenby et al.[51] of 893 individuals compared amfebutamone 300 mg/day for 9 weeks with transdermal nicotine 21 mg/24h for 6 weeks, followed by 14mg/24h and 7mg/24h for 1 week each; the combination of transdermal nicotine and amfebutamone; and placebo.[51] At 12 months, the point prevalence cessation rates were 35.5% for combination therapy and 30.3% for amfebutamone alone, both of which were significantly greater than the cessation rate for nicotine patch alone (16.4%) and placebo (15.6%). It is unclear why the cessation rates with nicotine patch were no greater than those seen with placebo, which is at variance with most other trials of nicotine patches.

Both of the above clinical trials excluded smokers with a current diagnosis of major depressive disorder. Further analysis of data from the trial by Hurt and colleagues[48] found that a past history of major depression or alcoholism had no influence on the efficacy of amfebutamone compared with placebo.[52] Also, the severity of depressive symptoms at baseline, as measured by the Beck Depression Inventory score, had no predictive value for the likelihood of cessation.

In both trials, amfebutamone resulted in less bodyweight gain in abstinent individuals during treatment compared with other treatment conditions, although at 6-months cessation differences in bodyweights were no longer significant. The study of Hurt et al.[48] found that amfebutamone did not reduce nicotine withdrawal scores, while that of Jorenby et al.[51] showed a reduction of withdrawal scores during the first 2 weeks of treatment.

Amfebutamone was moderately well tolerated, with the most common adverse effects being insomnia and dry mouth. In the study by Hurt et al.[48] discontinuation rates due to adverse reactions were 5 to 8% for amfebutamone-treated and 5% for placebo-treated individuals. In the study by Jorenby et al.[51] the rates were 11.9% for amfebutamone, 6.6% for nicotine patch, 11.4% for combined treatment and 3.8% for placebo.

Of note is that the past experience with immediate release amfebutamone as used for depression revealed a potential to produce seizures (0.1% at 300 mg/day or less and 0.4% at 450 mg/day) as well as hypertension. Seizures were dose-related and were more common in people with a seizure risk or predisposition (history of prior seizures, brain injury, alcoholism or sedative drug abuse) and in patients with eating disorders (anorexia nervosa or bulimia). However, no seizures were reported in the clinical trials for smoking cessation.

### 4.1.2 Nortriptyline

Nortriptyline, a tricyclic antidepressant (TCA), has similar effects to amfebutamone in that it increases noradrenaline levels by blocking reuptake and decreases firing in the locus ceruleus. Unlike amfebutamone, nortriptyline blocks serotonin reuptake, does not block dopamine reuptake, has anticholinergic effects and may be sedating.

Two clinical trials have demonstrated that nortriptyline is an effective aid to smoking cessation. Hall et al.[53] studied 199 smokers comparing, in a $2 \times 2$ design, nortriptyline versus placebo and cognitive-behavioural versus health education therapies.[53] Nortriptyline was selected among the TCAs because it is less sedating and therapeutic serum concentrations (at least for depression) are known. Individuals with a major depressive disorder within 3 months of onset of the trial were excluded, but 33% of participants had a past history of major depressive disorder. Nortriptyline was initiated at 25 mg/day for 3 days, then increased to 50 mg/day for 4 days. At week 2, serum concentrations were measured, and the drug increased to 75mg or 100mg per day, as necessary in order to achieve a therapeutic concentration. Nortriptyline was continued at full dose for 12 weeks, then tapered over 1 week. Smoking cessation was to begin at week 5 of nortriptyline therapy, so that adequate nortriptyline concentrations would have been achieved prior to cessation. Measurement of nortriptyline concentrations in abstinent smokers at week 6 indicated that only 51% had achieved serum concentrations that are therapeutic for depression.

Continuous abstinence rates were significantly higher with nortriptyline compared with placebo, with 24% continuous abstinence in those receiving nortriptyline versus 12% in those receiving placebo at 64 weeks [overall odds ratio (OR) 2.3, 95% confidence interval (CI) 1.1 to 1.5]. There was also a significant gender by history of depression interaction. Women with a past history of major depressive disorder had lower cessation rates compared with women who did not have such a history, but no such difference was seen in men. The benefit of nortriptyline treatment was independent of a history of major depressive disorder.

Nortriptyline treatment significantly reduced the Profile of Mood total mood disturbance score, which increased after smoking cessation in the placebo-treated smokers. Nortriptyline had no significant effect on overall nicotine withdrawal symptoms. Nortriptyline treatment was associated with an increased incidence of dry mouth, lightheadedness, shaky hands and blurred vision, but withdrawal rates from medication-induced adverse effects were low (4% on active drug versus 1% on placebo).

A second nortriptyline trial by Prochazka et al.[54] included 214 smokers randomised to nortriptyine or placebo treatment. Smokers with current major depressive disorder were excluded. 12% of those included had a past history of major depressive disorder. Nortriptyline was initiated at 25 mg/day for 3 days, then increased to 50 mg/day for 3 days and then, if tolerated, 75 mg/day. Smoking cessation occurred 10 days after initiating nortriptyline therapy. Nortriptyline was continued at the maximally tolerated dosage for 8 weeks, then tapered over the subsequent 2 weeks.

Nortriptyline treatment significantly enhanced continuous abstinence, with 6-month rates of 14% in nortriptyline-treated compared with 3% in placebo-treated smokers. Active treatment also significantly reduced withdrawal symptoms, including anxiety/tension and irritability/anger at 1 week after cessation, but did not significantly reduce craving or hunger and had no effect on Beck Depression scores. Adverse effects were observed more frequently in nortriptyline treated individuals, and included dry mouth, altered taste, drowsiness and gastrointestinal upset. Discontinuation due to adverse effects occurred in 9% of those receiving nortriptyline and 3% of those receiving placebo.

Whereas nortriptyline was generally well tolerated in these trials, the drug is well known to have serious and even lethal toxicity in overdose. There are also safety concerns about the use of TCAs in patients with cardiovascular disease.[55]

### 4.1.3 Doxepin

Doxepin, another TCA, was studied in a small placebo-controlled clinical trial (19 smokers).[56] Doxepin (150 mg/day) was administered 3 weeks before and 4 weeks after the target quit date. Point prevalence cessation at 9 weeks was significantly greater in the doxepin group (78%) compared with the placebo group (10%).

No follow-up studies have been reported. Based on this one small study, doxepin cannot at this time be recommended as a smoking cessation therapy.

### 4.1.4 Fluoxetine and Other Serotonin Reuptake Inhibitors

Fluoxetine is a selective serotonin reuptake inhibitor (SSRI). Because of the association between cigarette smoking and depression, fluoxetine has been studied as an aid to smoking cessation. As noted in section 3.1, there is also some evidence from animal studies that the reinforcing effects of nicotine are mediated in part by serotonin release.

A large trial of fluoxetine in smoking cessation was conducted in the 1980s, but the results of the main study were never published. A recent secondary analysis of that study suggested benefit in smoking cessation in smokers with symptoms of depression at baseline.[57]

Another study has been conducted involving 39 smokers with a history of major depression (but not currently depressed). Participants received fluoxetine 20 mg/day for 1 week, then 40 mg/day for 2 weeks, or placebo.[58] The study outcome was the severity of withdrawal symptoms. In those receiving fluoxetine, there was a significant decrease in tension, anger and depression, while no change over time was observed in the placebo group. This study suggested that fluoxetine might ameliorate some of the most bothersome symptoms experienced during smoking cessation (in smokers with a history of major depression).

A small treatment trial of 25 smokers with major depressive disorder and alcohol dependence compared fluoxetine 20 to 40 mg/day for 12 weeks with placebo.[59] Individuals taking fluoxetine smoked 27% fewer cigarettes and drank less alcohol compared with those receiving placebo, although the differences were not significant, as expected in such a small study.

In contrast with this study, other studies using fluoxetine in nondepressed individuals who were alcohol-dependent found no treatment effects on cigarette consumption.[60,61] Similar negative results were obtained using the SSRIs citalopram and zimeldine (zimelidine).[61]

Thus, preliminary data suggest that fluoxetine might be useful to aid smoking cessation in depressed smokers, but the results to date are inconsistent. Further research in depressed smokers, a difficult group in which to achieve smoking cessation, should be a high priority.

### 4.1.5 Moclobemide

The rationale for the use of MAO inhibitors (MAOIs) for smoking cessation is the link between smoking and depression, and the possibility that in depressed individuals smoking represents an attempt to self-medicate.

Moclobemide is a reversible MAO-A inhibitor which has been studied for smoking cessation in a group of 88 highly dependent smokers.[62] Of the study participants, 57% had a history of major depressive disorder, although none was taking antidepressant drugs at the time of the study. Moclobemide was administered at a dosage of 400 mg/ day for 1 week prior to the quit date, 400 mg/day for the next 2 months and then 200 mg/day for a third month, and was compared with placebo. At 6 months, the cotinine-verified cessation rates were higher in the moclobemide group (32% versus 16% in individuals receiving placebo), although this difference was not statistically significant.

Moclobemide did not relieve withdrawal symptoms and, in fact, insomnia was more frequent in the group taking moclobemide. Clinical depression did not develop in either group during withdrawal. The main adverse effects of moclobemide were insomnia and dry mouth. Rates of withdrawal from the study were similar in active and placebo treatment groups.

The current results must be viewed as preliminary and further trials with MAOIs are needed before this treatment can be advocated.

## 4.2 Clonidine

Clonidine was one of the first non-nicotine prescription medications evaluated for smoking cessation. Clonidine is an antihypertensive drug that acts in the brain both as an $\alpha_2$-adrenergic receptor agonist and as an imidazoline receptor agonist. Via its $\alpha_2$-agonist effects, clonidine inhibits the release of noradrenaline and inhibits the firing of the locus ceruleus, the result of which is sedation and anxiolysis.[63] The nicotine withdrawal syndrome may include symptoms such as tension and anxiety and drug craving, which are consistent with effects of locus ceruleus activation. It is presumed, but not proven, that clonidine aids smoking cessation by blocking the anxiety, irritability and drug craving which occur during nicotine withdrawal.

Clonidine was originally evaluated in a study of smoking withdrawal symptoms by Glassman et al.[64] The rationale for the study was to test whether the concept of noradrenergic involvement in opioid withdrawal could be extended to other appetitive behaviours, such as smoking. Subsequently, a number of trials have been performed on clonidine as an aid to smoking cessation. 10 double-blind studies with a sample size of 60 or more have been reported.[63,65] Clonidine, in dosages of 100 to 750 µg/day either orally or transdermally, typically started several days prior to cessation, has been compared with placebo. Most studies show a favourable trend for enhanced cessation with clonidine, although only one study found a significant effect at 6 months. This is most likely because the sample sizes were small. A meta-analysis of the four studies with a 6-month follow-up, involving 639 smokers, revealed a pooled OR of quitting of 2.0 (95% CI, 1.3 to 3.0) for clonidine versus placebo.[63] Cessation rates in these four trials ranged from 14 to 57% for clonidine- versus 11 to 37% for placebo-treated smokers.

Of interest was that four of 10 cessation studies reported trends toward greater efficacy in women compared with men.[63] Three of the studies reported that clonidine was ineffective in men. Glassman et al.[66] have reported a greater treatment effect in smokers with a higher level of dependence, and with a history of depression. In a trial of different doses of transdermal clonidine, Niaura et al.[65] found an interaction between the level of nicotine dependence, blood clonidine concentration and smoking cessation outcome. More dependent smokers ($\geq 7$ on Fagerström score) with higher blood clonidine concentrations had substantially better quit rates compared with those with lower clonidine concentrations. In contrast, quit rates in low dependence smokers were independent of the clonidine concentration achieved.

Clonidine has been reported to reduce craving, anxiety, irritability, restlessness and/or hunger in various studies.[63,65] Unfortunately, adverse effects, most notably sedation, dry mouth, dizziness and postural hypotension, are common with clonidine therapy. On average, 15% of individuals receiving clonidine compared with 8% of those receiving placebo discontinued therapy during clinical trials.

On balance, clonidine seems to be effective in reducing some tobacco withdrawal symptoms and promoting smoking cessation. The main problem with clonidine is its adverse effect profile. For this reason, clonidine cannot be considered first-line therapy. However, it should be considered for female smokers who experience extreme nicotine withdrawal symptoms, particularly agitation and anxiety, that are unrelieved by nicotine or amfebutamone. Clonidine may also be particularly useful in treating multiple drug abuse withdrawal, where drug abuse in addition to nicotine needs to be treated.[67]

A variety of clonidine dose and dose administration schedules have been described, but there has been no systematic research to determine which regimen is most effective. A suggested approach is to begin at 100μg twice a day (or an equivalent transdermal patch) and to titrate up to a maximum of 400 μg/day as needed and as tolerated. It has been recommended that clonidine be started 48 to 72 hours prior to cessation, if possible, although the drug could be added at any time for the treatment of severe withdrawal symptoms. Treatment studies have typically lasted for 3 or 4 weeks, followed by a tapering of clonidine to avoid withdrawal effects from the cessation of clonidine itself. Clonidine withdrawal symptoms include anxiety, tremulousness, agitation and tachycardia.

### 4.3 Buspirone

Buspirone, a nonbenzodiazepine anxiolytic drug, is believed to work primarily as a serotonin $5\text{-HT}_{1A}$ receptor partial agonist, but also increases firing rates of dopaminergic and noradrenergic neurons. It has been studied in several clinical trials of smoking cessation; the rationale for studying buspirone was that it might reduce the anxiety and other dysphoric aspects of nicotine withdrawal, while being nonsedating and having a relatively low abuse potential.

West et al.[68] treated 61 smokers with buspirone 15 mg/day or placebo for 2 weeks prior to attempted abstinence, and then for 4 weeks after the quit date. Continuous abstinence (carbon monoxide-confirmed) at 4 weeks was significantly greater in the buspirone (47%) than the placebo (16%) group. In this study, buspirone did not significantly reduce withdrawal symptoms.

Robinson et al.[69] treated 54 smokers with buspirone (30 mg/day) or placebo for 3 weeks before abrupt cessation of tobacco use. There were no significant effects of buspirone on withdrawal symptoms or on cessation rate. In contrast, Hilleman et al.[70] found that buspirone 30 mg/day for 3 weeks prior to and 1 week after smoking cessation reduced craving, anxiety, irritability and restlessness to a greater extent than placebo (n = 40). There were no treatment effects on hunger, impaired concentration and drowsiness associated with smoking cessation. No long term follow-up data were presented.

Cinciripini et al.[71] reported a study of 101 smokers who received buspirone (up to 60 mg/day) or placebo for 4 weeks prior to and 4 weeks following the target quit day. All individuals received cognitive-behavioural therapy. Buspirone enhanced the rate of abstinence (point prevalence, confirmed by carbon monoxide and cotinine measurements) during treatment, although the benefits were only seen in smokers with high levels of anxiety (abstinence rates at the end of therapy: buspirone 88%, placebo 61%.). Smokers with low levels of anxiety seemed to do worse on buspirone (buspirone 60%, placebo 89%). Buspirone had no effect on long term abstinence, and no effect on withdrawal symptoms was observed.

In a recent study by Schneider et al.,[72] 100 smokers received buspirone 25 to 30 mg/day or placebo for 3 weeks prior to cessation and then remained on the drug for 6 weeks after cessation.[72] Patients were followed to 1 year. Buspirone had no effect on tobacco abstinence or the severity of withdrawal symptoms.

Overall, the studies do not support the use of buspirone as a first-line drug for smoking cessation. However, there may be an adjunctive role for buspirone in treating a subset of smokers with high levels of anxiety prior to smoking cessation.

### 4.4 Mecamylamine

Mecamylamine is a noncompetitive nicotinic receptor antagonist that appears to act by sterically blocking cationic conductance through the receptor ion channel, and may also act as an allosteric inhibitor, decreasing the density of nicotine binding sites.[28,29] Mecamylamine is lipid soluble and easily penetrates the brain, blocking CNS nicotine receptors. It also acts as an autonomic ganglionic blocker in the peripheral nervous system, an effect which is responsible for its adverse effects.

The rationale for receptor antagonist therapy is to produce a condition in which the recipient becomes insensitive to the reinforcing effects of a drug. For example, naltrexone, an opioid receptor antagonist, is used in the treatment of detoxified opioid abusers and is effective in reducing relapse to opioids.[67]

Mecamylamine has been shown to block the behavioural effects of nicotine in animals.[73] In contrast, quaternary ganglionic nicotinic receptor blocking drugs such as hexamethonium, which do not enter the brain, do not have such an effect. Experimental studies in humans have shown that mecamylamine alone given orally (7.5 to 22.5mg) to smokers acutely increases cigarette consumption.[31,74] Increased smoking is felt to be a compensatory response to the reduced satisfaction derived from nicotine in the cigarette smoke. This is supported by reports that cigarettes are perceived as less strong and less satisfying when taken with mecamylamine.[74,75] Mecamylamine has also been shown to eliminate the 'drug liking' response to intravenous nicotine.[76] Other studies have shown that pretreatment with mecamylamine increased plasma nicotine concentrations after smoking individual cigarettes, supporting the idea of a compensatory effort.[30]

A small, uncontrolled trial of mecamylamine alone to aid smoking cessation found that an average dose of 27mg reduced craving for cigarettes and suggested a benefit in aiding quitting.[77] However, serious adverse effects were common. These adverse effects may include orthostatic hypotension, blurred vision, dry mouth, constipation, abdominal discomfort and/or urinary retention. The potential toxicity of mecamylamine used alone tempered early enthusiasm for the use of this drug. Of interest, is the observation that mecamylamine does not appear to precipitate acute nicotine withdrawal symptoms in smokers, as naloxone and naltrexone do in opioid-dependent individuals.[78]

The work of Rose and Levin[79] has recently rekindled interest in mecamylamine, when used in combination with nicotine, to aid smoking cessation. The rationale for the combination is that nicotine and mecamylamine might act in concert to reduce the positive reinforcing effects of nicotine from cigarette smoke, while nicotine would prevent withdrawal symptoms and diminish the potential adverse effects of peripheral ganglionic blockade produced by mecamylamine.

A small clinical trial was performed in which smokers received mecamylamine 10 mg/day orally for 2 weeks prior to the planned quit date in addition to transdermal nicotine 21 mg/day, started either at the same time as mecamylamine or 2 weeks later at the quit date.[32] The comparison group received transdermal nicotine and placebo capsules. Mecamylamine was continued for 3 weeks after smoking cessation, and transdermal nicotine was continued, with a gradual tapering of dose, for 6 weeks after cessation.

At 7 weeks after the quit date, continuous abstinence rates were 50% for the mecamylamine-nicotine group versus 17% for the transdermal nicotine alone group. Early compared with late initiation of transdermal nicotine had no influence on quit rate. Mecamylamine and nicotine in combination reduced the craving for cigarettes, even prior to the quit date. Mecamylamine-nicotine reduced negative affect (defined as self-reported tension and irritability) and appetite during abstinence. Cigarette smoking decreased substantially in the mecamylamine-nicotine group prior to the quit date, with little if any effect of nicotine patch therapy alone. The combination was well tolerated. Only 3 of 24 individuals receiving the combination experienced severe adverse effects from mecamylamine (constipation, abdominal pain) which required a reduction of the dosage from 10 to 5 mg/day. Mild constipation was noted in 70% of the mecamylamine recipients versus 32% of placebo recipients, and in some cases necessitated treatment with over-the-counter (OTC) laxatives.

A second small trial by Rose et al.[75] compared transdermal nicotine plus mecamylamine (5mg twice a day), nicotine alone (24 mg/24h), mecamylamine alone or no active drug administered for 4 weeks prior to cessation. Subsequently, all individuals received nicotine plus mecamylamine for 6 weeks, followed by 2 weeks of tapering dosages of transdermal nicotine. The nicotine and mecamylamine conditions decreased smoking satisfaction and *ad libitum* smoking rates prior to quitting (the latter from an average of 30 to 15 cigarettes per day). Precessation mecamylamine treatment, with or without nicotine, significantly enhanced continuous abstinence rates for 6 to 9 weeks after cessation. The authors speculate that the increased duration of abstinence during mecamylamine therapy administered precessation is due to attenuation of the reinforcing effects of nicotine during *ad libitum* cigarette smoking.

Finally, a recent abstract reported a preliminary analysis of 252 individuals showing an interaction between gender and precessation mecamylamine treatment.[80] As with other mecamylamine trials, study participants received transdermal nicotine after the quit date. Women benefitted more from mecamylamine than men. The cessation rates at 7 weeks post-treatment, comparing mecamylamine versus placebo, were 34 versus 17% for women and 30 versus 25% for men.

In summary, mecamylamine has the potential to block the reinforcing effects of cigarette smoking and, as such, holds considerable promise as an aid to smoking cessation. Mecamylamine alone acutely increases smoking rates as smokers attempt to overcome reduced reinforcement, and so does not appear to be useful for smoking cessation. However, long term administration of mecamylamine combined with nicotine and initiated prior to cessation decreases *ad libitum* smoking rates, presumably reflecting the extinction of reinforcement over time. Preliminary data suggest that such treatment may enhance quitting rates. Adding nicotine to mecamylamine also reduces the adverse effects of mecamylamine, although some adverse effects, particularly constipation, may still be problematic. Larger trials of mecamylamine combined with nicotine in a transdermal delivery system are ongoing, and should clarify the utility, optimal doses and timing of mecamylamine treatment, and the adverse effects and role of such therapy in the smoking cessation armamentarium.

## 4.5 Sensory Stimulants

Sensory responses to smoking, including responses within the respiratory tract, become associated with the pharmacological effects of nicotine and become a reinforcing aspect of smoking. Nicotine is an irritant to the respiratory tract, and the perceived 'strength' (which includes the sensation of irritation) of cigarette smoke is a good predictor of nicotine dose.[81] Sensory factors appear to play a role in regulating the intake of cigarette smoke. Sensory stimulants, including ascorbic acid and citric acid, have been evaluated as adjuncts to smoking cessation therapy. The rationale is that these treatments will substitute for some of the sensory aspects of smoking, thereby reducing the cigarette craving related to conditioned responses.

An ascorbic acid aerosol delivery device has been tested in small clinical trials. One trial used a cigarette-sized tube that released a fine powder of ascorbic acid, which reproduced some of the sensations produced by cigarette smoking.[82] 63 smokers were administered an ascorbic acid inhaler following 2 weeks of smoking cigarettes with reduced nicotine yield. They were allowed to use the ascorbic acid device for up to 12 weeks. All smokers received behavioural counselling. Individuals using the ascorbic acid device had substantially greater chances of continuous abstinence at 3 weeks than those receiving only behavioural counselling (60 *vs* 22%). Of note, ascorbic acid increased the craving for cigarettes on day 8 of cessation, raising the possibility that sensory stimulation may interfere with the extinguishing of reinforcement that naturally occurs after smoking cessation.

Another sensory stimulation trial used a hand-held citric acid inhaler in 74 smokers.[37] Study participants were instructed to use the inhaler whenever they had an urge to smoke after the quit date – for as long as 12 days. Abstinence at 19 days after the quit date was significantly greater in citric acid-treated individuals who had high baseline carbon monoxide levels (presumably reflecting more dependent smokers) but not in those with low baseline carbon monoxide levels (less dependent smokers).

Most recently, a trial compared citric acid or placebo inhalers for 10 weeks combined with transdermal nicotine for 6 weeks.[83] Continuous abstinence rates at 10 weeks were 19.5% for citric acid plus nicotine patch versus 6.8% for nicotine patch alone (p = 0.05). The inhaler also reduced craving and some abstinence symptoms. At 6 months, however, there was no significant difference between treatment groups.

Inhalation of vapour of black pepper oil, which produces respiratory tract symptoms similar to that of smoking, reduced cigarette craving and some nicotine withdrawal symptoms in smokers after overnight abstinence from cigarettes.[84] We are not aware of any clinical trials using pepper extract to aid cessation.

In summary, these studies suggest that the use of sensory stimulants to simulate the sensation of cigarette smoking may reduce craving and some withdrawal symptoms. When combined with nicotine or other pharmacotherapy, sensory stimulants might enhance smoking cessation rates. Work is ongoing to develop sensory stimulants with improved particle size and delivery characteristics.

### 4.6 Silver Acetate

Silver acetate has been available as an OTC smoking deterrent in the form of chewing gum, lozenges and spray. The silver in this product reacts with cigarette smoke to form an unpleasant metallic taste, which is the basis for this aversive therapy. Several clinical trials of silver acetate that include verification of smoking status have been published.

Malcolm et al.[85] compared silver acetate (6mg) gum (marketed in Europe as 'Tabmit') versus placebo in 282 smokers. Patients were instructed to chew 6 pieces of gum per day for 3 weeks, with quitting to occur between 8 and 17 days of use. No behavioural therapy was provided. Carbon monoxide-confirmed point prevalence quit rates were 11 and 4% for silver acetate versus placebo (p < 0.05) at 3 weeks (end of treatment) and 7 versus 3% at 4 months (nonsignificant).

Jensen and co-workers[86] studied silver acetate chewing gum compared with nicotine gum or ordinary chewing gum in 495 smokers. Silver acetate gum was limited to 6 pieces of gum per day, while nicotine and placebo gums could be used *ad libitum* for up to 12 weeks. The dose of silver acetate gum was limited to avoid argyria, a condition in which excessive intake of silver produces bluing of the skin. A series of smoking cessation counselling sessions were held. Patients were stratified based on their pack-year smoking history. Overall, there were no significant differences in cessation rates for the three treatments. However, a subset analysis of smokers with low pack-year history (presumably reflecting a lower level of dependence) found that these individuals were more likely to quit (74%) than those with high pack-year history (28%) [point prevalence confirmed by carbon monoxide measurement] at 6 months using silver acetate. No such differences were seen with nicotine or ordinary gum.

Morrow et al.[87] studied 42 smokers who received a silver acetate or placebo mouth spray, to be used every 2 hours for 3 weeks. No significant effects on quit rates were observed. Hymowitz and Eckholdt[88] studied a 2.5mg silver acetate lozenge versus placebo in 500 smokers. Patients were given brief behavioural counselling and were instructed to use the lozenge every 2 hours but not more than 6 times per day for 3 weeks. Initial (3-week) point prevalence quit rates were 17 and 11% for silver acetate and placebo, respectively (a nonsignificant difference). Quit rate differences were significant if only individuals who used the lozenges were analysed. At 12 weeks, cessation rates were similar (4%) for both groups.

Taken as a whole, these studies suggest that silver acetate may have some efficacy in the short term, and particularly in lighter smokers. The problem, of course, is that when a person has a strong craving to smoke, it is easy to discontinue use of the silver acetate rather than not smoke. Silver acetate cannot be recommended as an effective pharmacotherapy for smoking cessation.

## 4.7 Other Therapies

### 4.7.1 Opioid Antagonists

Nicotine causes the release of endogenous opioid peptides in the CNS, and it has been suggested that this action may contribute to the reinforcing effects of nicotine.[89] Naloxone has been reported to precipitate withdrawal symptoms in nicotine-treated rodents and in human smokers.[90,91]

The effects of opioid antagonists on cigarette smoking have been studied, both to elucidate how opioid systems modulate smoking behaviour and to determine if opioid antagonists might be useful aids to smoking cessation. Two small studies have reported that naloxone, a short-acting opioid antagonist, at a dose of 10mg, reduced *ad libitum* smoking compared with placebo treatment in brief test sessions.[92,93] Another study of varying doses of naloxone found, however, no effect on smoking behaviour.[94] A fourth study found that naltrexone, a long-acting opioid antagonist, had no effect on cigarette consumption or nicotine intake over 48 hours.[95]

A clinical trial of 100 smokers compared naltrexone 50 mg/day or placebo for 12 weeks, with or without transdermal nicotine.[96] Continuous abstinence rates at the end of treatment showed significant effects for transdermal nicotine only. Cessation rates were 36% for trans-dermal nicotine plus placebo, 31% for transdermal nicotine plus naltrexone, 12% for placebo alone and 9% for naltrexone only. Naltrexone had no effects on cessation rates. Transdermal nicotine reduced craving and *ad libitum* cigarette smoking in smokers who did not quit, but naltrexone had no such effects. Furthermore, naltrexone treatment was associated with a higher rate of headache, and the 3 participants who terminated the study prematurely because of adverse drug reactions were taking naltrexone (although 2 were also taking nicotine).

Thus, the clinical trial data to date do not suggest a role for opioid antagonists as adjuncts to smoking cessation therapy.

### 4.7.2 Corticotropin

Corticotropin has been proposed as a treatment to aid smoking cessation, based on the hypothesis that nicotine increases corticotropin and cortisol release and that during nicotine withdrawal there may be a state of hypoadrenocorticism. Uncontrolled studies of small numbers of smokers administered 2 or 3 corticotropin injections in the first week of cessation have reported high cessation rates and/or substantial reduction in cigarette consumption.[97,98] These are not controlled studies, however, and cessation rates were not biochemically verified. In the absence of controlled clinical trials, corticotropin cannot be recommended.

### 4.7.3 Lobeline

Lobeline is a nonpyridine alkaloid found in Indian tobacco (*Lobelia inflata*). It increases dopamine levels by inhibiting dopamine reuptake by synaptic vesicles.[99] Lobeline binds with high affinity to some nicotinic cholinergic receptors but does not activate $\alpha_4 \beta_2$ receptors, which are predominant in the brain.[100] Its dopamine-releasing properties do not appear to be

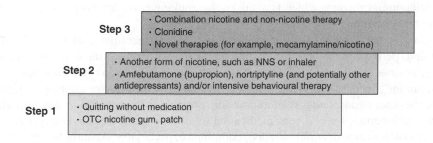

**Fig. 4.** Stepped care approach to smoking cessation therapy. Recommendations are based on the opinions of the authors. Empirical data to support these recommendations are not available. **NNS** = nicotine nasal spray; **OTC** = over-the-counter.

mediated by nicotinic receptor activation. Lobeline is reported to have some nicotine-like activity and has been used as a type of nicotine substitution therapy. Some older reports have suggested benefit,[101-103] but other studies (including a recent unpublished clinical trial) have not confirmed efficacy.[104,105] On balance, there appears to be no role for lobeline in smoking cessation.

## 5. The Place of Non-Nicotine Pharmacotherapy in Smoking Cessation

Nicotine medications have been the mainstay of the pharmacotherapy of smoking cessation until very recently.[1] While they have been extremely useful, quit rates remain disappointingly low. The availability of non-nicotine medications expands the options, and a greater variety of therapeutic options offers a potentially greater likelihood of successful cessation for more smokers. A proposed stepped care approach for the selection of pharmacotherapy for smoking cessation (based on the judgment of the authors rather than empirical data) is presented in figure 4.

Since nicotine maintains tobacco use and tobacco is easily and inexpensively available, it makes sense for NRT to be readily available and affordable. Towards this end, nicotine polacrilex gum and transdermal nicotine have been made available OTC in the US and many other countries, and in some countries nicotine inhalers are also available OTC. Most smokers have tried to quit multiple times before they seek professional assistance. It seems appropriate to recommend that smokers try to quit using OTC nicotine therapies initially. Cessation rates with the use of OTC NRTs average only about 10%, but this rate is still twice as high as the cessation rate seen with OTC placebo therapy.[4] Smokers who fail to quit using OTC nicotine therapy, who are likely to be the more dependent smokers, should seek medical care for further therapy.

Once a smoker has failed a trial of nicotine patch therapy (assuming that he or she has complied with proper doses and dose duration, which is often not the case with the use of OTC medications), the likelihood of responding to a second course of the same therapy is low.[106] Thus, the clinician has the option of recommending another type of NRT or a non-nicotine medication. Another important option, which may be pursued with and without medication, is group behavioural therapy, which is available in smoking cessation clinics within many medical centres or community clinics.

Options for prescription nicotine medications include nicotine nasal spray, the nicotine inhaler and, perhaps in the near future, nicotine lozenges and nicotine oral transmucosal delivery systems (lollipops). Currently available non-nicotine medications include amfebutamone (the only non-nicotine therapy approved by the FDA for smoking cessation) and some of the other antidepressants, clonidine and, possibly in the near future, a mecamylamine-nicotine combination. The choice of medication should depend on the individual patient, including factors such as ease of administration, compliance, psychiatric comorbidity, and particular vulnerabilities to adverse effects of different therapies.

The tolerability of both NRT and amfebutamone seems to be excellent. Many smokers as well as physicians believe that nicotine is dangerous and that medications containing nicotine should be avoided or at least used for as short a time as possible. Although there was concern in 1992 that nicotine patches might cause heart attacks, recent clinical trials and experimental studies suggest that nicotine does not have clinically significant adverse cardiovascular effects, even in people with heart disease who take nicotine while continuing to smoke.[107,108] There is no evidence that nicotine causes cancer. Nicotine could theoretically contribute to adverse outcomes of pregnancy, including fetal neurotoxicity, although no safety data on NRT are available to determine whether this is a significant risk.[109] People can also become dependent on NRT, an effect that seems to be related to the rate of nicotine absorption by the body. Thus, the risk of dependence is expected to be greatest with nicotine nasal spray, less with nicotine gum and nil with nicotine patches.

Like nicotine, amfebutamone has some sympathomimetic actions. Few data are available on the safety of the drug in smokers with coronary heart disease or in pregnant smokers. In excessive doses, but occasionally at therapeutic doses, amfebutamone can cause anxiety or can worsen panic and anxiety disorders, and produce hypertension and, rarely, seizures. Nortriptyline, and other TCAs, can have serious anticholinergic adverse effects and overdose is potentially lethal. Amfebutamone and nortriptyline probably pose little or no risk of dependence. Because of the bothersome adverse effects of sedation and postural hypotension, clonidine should be reserved as a third-line therapy for the treatment of smokers with severe withdrawal symptoms, especially anxiety and agitation.

Finally, there is the possibility of combining nicotine and non-nicotine medications. New medications such as the mecamylamine-nicotine combination, when it becomes available, will be one such combination therapy. As noted in section 4.1.1, a combination of transdermal nicotine and amfebutamone may be more effective than either drug alone. This may be the case when combining other nicotine with non-nicotine therapies as well.

## 6. Future Prospects

As we learn more about the neurochemistry of nicotine addiction, new pharmacological approaches to aid smoking cessation will undoubtedly emerge.

The future of pharmacotherapy for smoking cessation is likely to include the use of nicotine receptor subtype–specific agonists and antagonists. The brain nicotine receptor is composed of $\alpha$ and $\beta$ subunits.[19] There are at least seven different $\alpha$ and three different $\beta$ subunits that may be present in various combinations in nicotine brain receptors. Different receptor subtypes have different affinities for nicotinic agonists, different electrophysiological responses to stimulation, and probably modulate different neurochemical release patterns. It is likely that different nicotinic receptor subtypes mediate different nicotine actions, including actions on behaviour and mood.

It may be possible to develop nicotine subtype-specific agonists and antagonists that have highly selective nicotine-like psychoactivity without cardiovascular or other potential adverse effects. Some nicotine analogues that selectively activate specific nicotinic receptor subtypes have been developed, and some are in clinical testing.[110,111] In an ideal pharmacotherapeutic milieu, the individual characteristics of smokers related to their particular reinforcements and/or withdrawal symptoms would be identified, and specific nicotinic receptor agonists and/or antagonists would be prescribed to provide selective reinforcement and/or amelioration of particular withdrawal symptoms, without affecting other nicotinic processes.

Another intriguing prospect is the induction of antibodies to nicotine by vaccination. Circulating antibodies could in theory bind nicotine in the circulation, thereby preventing it reaching the brain and, therefore, blocking its reinforcing actions. Immunisation would be functionally equivalent to administration of a receptor antagonist that prevents nicotine access to the receptor. Antibodies have been induced by immunisation of rats with nicotine linked to an immunogen.[112,113] After a particular dose of nicotine, immunised animals have markedly higher blood nicotine concentrations compared with non-immunised animals, owing to binding of nicotine by antibodies in the plasma.[112,113] Immunisation reduced brain nicotine concentrations following multiple doses of intravenous nicotine by 30 to 46%.[113] Whether this magnitude of reduction of nicotine concentration in the brain will alter the reinforcing effects of nicotine remains to be determined, but is a reasonable supposition.

The feasibility of immunotherapy for nicotine dependence is supported by animal studies in which active immunisation against cocaine or passive administration of cocaine-specific antibodies resulted in a reduction of brain concentrations of cocaine of a similar magnitude to that observed for nicotine, and was associated with reduced locomotor responses and suppressed self-administration of cocaine.[114,115]

In conclusion, research in recent years has tremendously expanded our understanding of nicotine addiction. The challenge of the future is to translate knowledge of the biology of nicotine addiction into pharmacological therapies that target individual differences in reinforcement in addicted smokers. To do so will require the development of new drugs, as well as clinical research attempting to match particular therapies to particular smokers.

## Acknowledgements

Preparation of this manuscript was supported in part by US Public Health Service grants DA02277 and DA01696 from the National Institute on Drug Abuse, National Institutes of Health.

## References

1. Henningfield JE. Nicotine medications for smoking cessation. N Engl J Med 1995; 333: 1196-7
2. Sutherland G, Stapleton JA, Russell MAH, et al. Randomised controlled trial of nasal nicotine spray in smoking cessation. Lancet 1992; 340: 324-9
3. Tonnesen P, Nørregaard J, Simonsen K, et al. A double-blind trial of a 16-hour transdermal nicotine patch in smoking cessation. N Engl J Med 1991; 325: 311-5
4. Hughes JR, Goldstein MG, Hurt RD, et al. Recent advances in the pharmacotherapy of smoking. JAMA 1999; 281: 72-6
5. Borrelli B, Niaura R, Keuthen NJ, et al. Development of major depressive disorder during smoking-cessation treatment. J Clin Psychiatry 1996; 57: 534-8
6. Shiffman S, Paty JA, Gnys M, et al. First lapses to smoking: within-subjects analysis of real-time reports. J Consult Clin Psychol 1996; 64: 366-79

7.   Russell MAH, Jarvis MJ. Theoretical background and clinical use of nicotine chewing gum. In: Grabowski J, Hall SH, Grabowski J, et al., editors. Pharmacological adjuncts in smoking cessation. Washington, DC: U.S. Govt. Printing Office, 1985: 110-30

8.   Palmer KJ, Buckley MM, Faulds D. Transdermal nicotine. A review of its pharmacodynamic and pharmacokinetic properties, and therapeutic efficacy as an aid to smoking cessation. Drugs 1992; 44: 498-529

9.   Gross J, Stitzer M. Nicotine replacement: ten-week effects on tobacco withdrawal symptoms. Psychopharmacology 1989; 98: 334-41

10.  Dale LC, Schroeder DR, Wolter TD, et al. Weight change after smoking cessation using variable doses of transdermal nicotine replacement. J Gen Intern Med 1998; 13: 9-15

11.  Wonnacott S. The paradox of nicotinic acetylcholine receptor upregulation by nicotine. Trends Pharmacol Sci 1990; 11 (6): 216-9

12.  Balfour DJK, Fagerstrom KO. Pharmacology of nicotine and its therapeutic use in smoking cessation and neurodegenerative disorders. Pharmacol Ther 1996; 72: 51-81

13.  Fattinger K, Verotta D, Benowitz NL. Pharmacodynamics of acute tolerance to multiple nicotinic effects in humans. J Pharmacol Exp Ther 1997; 281: 1238-46

14.  Balfour DJ. Neural mechanisms underlying nicotine dependence. Addiction 1994; 89: 1419-23

15.  Foulds J, Stapleton J, Feyerabend C, et al. Effect of transdermal nicotine patches on cigarette smoking: a double blind crossover study. Psychopharmacology 1992; 106: 421-7

16.  Levin ED, Westman EC, Stein RM, et al. Nicotine skin patch treatment increases abstinence, decreases withdrawal symptoms, and attenuates rewarding effects of smoking. J Clin Psychopharmacol 1994; 14: 41-9

17.  Olale F, Gerzanich V, Kuryatov A, et al. Chronic nicotine exposure differentially affects the function of human $\alpha3$, $\alpha4$, and $\alpha7$ neuronal nicotinic receptor subtypes. J Pharmacol Exp Ther 1997; 283: 675-83

18.  Benowitz NL. Pharmacology of nicotine: addiction and therapeutics. Annu Rev Pharmacol Toxicol 1996; 36: 597-613

19.  McGehee DS, Role LW. Physiological diversity of nicotinic acetylcholine receptors expressed by vertebrate neurons. Annu Rev Physiol 1995; 57: 521-46

20.  Di Chiara G. The role of dopamine in drug abuse viewed from the perspective of its role in motivation. Drug Alcohol Depend 1995; 38: 95-137

21.  Pontieri FE, Tanda G, Orzi F, et al. Effects of nicotine on the nucleus accumbens and similarity to those of addictive drugs. Nature 1996; 382: 255-7

22.  Corrigall WA, Coen KM, Adamson KL. Self-administered nicotine activates the mesolimbic dopamine system through the ventral tegmental area. Brain Res 1994; 653: 278-84

23.  Grenhoff J, Svensson TH. Pharmacology of nicotine. Br J Addict 1989; 84: 477-92

24.  Matta SG, Singh J, Sharp BM. Catecholamines mediate nicotine-induced adrenocorticotropin secretion via alpha-adrenergic receptors. Endocrinology 1990; 127: 1646-55

25.  Benwell MEM, Balfour DJK, Anderson JM. Smoking-related changes in the serotonergic systems of discrete regions of human brain. Psychopharmacology 1990; 102: 68-72

26.  Bianchi C, Ferraro L, Tanganelli S, et al. 5-Hydroxytryptamine-mediated effects of nicotine on endogenous GABA efflux from guinea-pig cortical slices. Br J Pharmacol 1995; 116: 2724-8

27.  Carboni E, Acquas E, Leone P, et al. 5-HT$_3$ receptor antagonists block morphine- and nicotine- but not amphetamine-induced reward. Psychopharmacology (Berl) 1989; 97: 175-8

28.  Martin BR, Onaivi ES, Martin TJ. What is the nature of mecamylamine's antagonism of the central effects of nicotine? Biochem Pharmacol 1989; 38: 3391-7

29.  Takayama H, Majewska MD, London ED. Interactions of noncompetitive inhibitors with nicotinic receptors in the rat brain. J Pharmacol Exp Ther 1989; 253: 1083-9

30.  Pomerleau CS, Pomerleau OF, Majchrzak MJ. Mecamylamine pretreatment increases subsequent nicotine self-administration as indicated by changes in plasma nicotine level. Psychopharmacology 1987; 91: 391-3

31.  Nemeth-Coslett R, Henningfield JE, O'Keefe MK, et al. Effects of mecamylamine on human cigarette smoking and subjective ratings. Psychopharmacology 1986; 88: 420-5

32.  Rose JE, Behm FM, Westman EC, et al. Mecamylamine combined with nicotine skin patch facilitates smoking cessation beyond nicotine patch treatment alone. Clin Pharmacol Ther 1994; 56: 86-99

33.  Fryer JD, Lukas RJ. Noncompetitive functional inhibition at diverse, human nicotinic acetylcholine receptor subtypes by bupropion, phencyclidine, and ibogaine. J Pharmacol Exp Ther 1999; 288: 88-92

34.  Fryer JD, Lukas RJ. Antidepressants noncompetitively inhibit nicotinic acetylcholine receptor function. J Neurochem 1999; 72: 1117-24

35.  Benowitz NL. Pharmacologic aspects of cigarette smoking and nicotine addiction. N Engl J Med 1988; 319: 1318-30

36.  Westman EC, Behm FM, Rose JE. Dissociating the nicotine and airway sensory effects of smoking cessation. Pharmacol Biochem Behav 1996; 53: 309-15

37.  Behm FM, Schur C, Levin ED, et al. Clinical evaluation of a citric acid inhaler for smoking cessation. Drug Alcohol Depend 1993; 31: 131-8

38.  Butschky MF, Bailey D, Henningfield JE, et al. Smoking without nicotine delivery decreases withdrawal in 12-hour abstinent smokers. Pharmacol Biochem Behav 1994; 50: 91-6

39.  Anda RF, Williamson DF, Escobedo LG, et al. Depression and the dynamics of smoking: a national perspective. JAMA 1990; 264: 1541-5

40.  Hall SM, Munoz RF, Reus VI, et al. Nicotine, negative affect and depression. J Consult Clin Psychol 1993; 61: 761-7

41.  Glassman AH, Helzer JE, Covey LS, et al. Smoking, smoking cessation and major depression. JAMA 1990; 264: 1546-9

42. Covey LS, Glassman AH, Stetner F. Depression and depressive symptoms in smoking cessation. Compr Psychiatry 1990; 31: 350-4

43. Fowler JS, Volkow ND, Wang GJ, et al. Inhibition of monoamine oxidase B in the brains of smokers. Nature 1996; 379: 733-7

44. Fowler JS, Volkow ND, Wang GJ, et al. Brain monoamine oxidase A inhibition in cigarette smokers. Proc Natl Acad Sci U S A 1996; 93: 14065-9

45. Kendler KS, Neale MC, MacLean CJ, et al. Smoking and major depression: a causal analysis. Arch Gen Psychiatry 1993; 50: 36-43

46. Ascher JA, Cole JO, Colin JN, et al. Bupropion: a review of its mechanism of antidepressant activity. J Clin Psychiatry 1995; 56: 395-401

47. Cooper BR, Wang CM, Cox RF, et al. Evidence that the acute behavioral and electrophysiological effects of bupropion (Wellbutrin®) are mediated by a noradrenergic mechanism. Neuropsychopharmacology 1994; 11: 133-41

48. Hurt RD, Sachs DPL, Glover ED, et al. A comparison of sustained release bupropion and placebo. N Engl J Med 1997; 337: 1195-202

49. Ferry LH, Robbins AS, Scarlati PD, et al. Enhancement of smoking cessation using the antidepressant, bupropion hydrochloride [abstract]. Circulation 1992; 86: I-671

50. Ferry LH, Burchette RJ. Efficacy of bupropion for smoking cessation in non-depressed smokers. J Addict Dis 1994; 13: 249

51. Jorenby DE, Leischow SJ, Nides MA, et al. A controlled trial of sustained-release bupropion, a nicotine patch, or both for smoking cessation. N Engl J Med 1999; 340: 685-91

52. Hayford KE, Patten CA, Rummans TA, et al. Efficacy of bupropion for smoking cessation in smokers with a former history of major depression or alcoholism. Br J Psychiatry 1999; 174: 173-8

53. Hall SM, Reus VI, Munoz RF, et al. Nortriptyline and cognitive-behavioral therapy in the treatment of cigarette smoking. Arch Gen Psychiatry 1998; 55: 683-90

54. Prochazka AV, Weaver MJ, Keller RT, et al. A randomized trial of nortriptyline for smoking cessation. Arch Intern Med 1998; 158: 2035-9

55. Glassman AH, Roose SP, Bigger JT. The safety of tricyclic antidepressants in cardiac patients. JAMA 1993; 269: 2673-5

56. Edwards NB, Murphy JK, Downs AD, et al. Doxepin as an adjunct to smoking cessation: a double-blind pilot study. Am J Psychiatry 1989; 146: 373-6

57. Niaura R, Goldstein MG, Depue J, et al. Fluoxetine, symptoms of depression, and smoking cessation [abstract]. Ann Behav Med 1995; 17: Suppl.: S061

58. Dalack GW, Glassman AH, Rivelli S, et al. Mood, major depression and fluoxetine response in cigarette smokers. Am J Psychiatry 1995; 152: 398-403

59. Cornelius JR, Salloum IM, Ehler JG, et al. Double-blind fluoxetine in depressed alcoholic smokers. Psychopharmacol Bull 1997; 33: 165-70

60. Naranjo CA, Kadlec KE, Sanheuza P, et al. Fluoxetine differentially alters alcohol intake and other consummatory behaviors in problem drinkers. Clin Pharmacol Ther 1990; 47: 490-8

61. Sellers EM, Naranjo CA, Kadlec K. Do serotonin uptake inhibitors decrease smoking? Observations in a group of heavy drinkers. J Clin Psychopharmacol 1987; 7: 417-20

62. Berlin I, Said S, Spreux-Varoquaux O, et al. A reversible monoamine oxidase A inhibitor (moclobemide) facilitates smoking cessation and abstinence in heavy, dependent smokers. Clin Pharmacol Ther 1995; 58: 444-52

63. Gourlay SG, Benowitz NL. Is clonidine an effective smoking cessation therapy? Drugs 1995; 50: 197-207

64. Glassman AH, Jackson WK, Walsh BT, et al. Cigarette craving, smoking withdrawal and clonidine. Science 1984; 226: 864-6

65. Niaura R, Brown RA, Goldstein MG, et al. Transdermal clonidine for smoking cessation: a double-blind randomized dose-response study. Exp Clin Psychopharmacol 1996; 4: 285-91

66. Glassman AH, Covey LS, Dalack GW, et al. Smoking cessation, clonidine, and vulnerability to nicotine among dependent smokers. Clin Pharmacol Ther 1993; 54: 670-9

67. Gold MS. Opiate addiction and the locus coeruleus. Psychiatr Clin North Am 1993; 16: 61-73

68. West R, Hajek P, McNeill A. Effect of buspirone on cigarette withdrawal symptoms and short-term abstinence rates in a smokers clinic. Psychopharmacology 1991; 104: 91-6

69. Robinson MD, Pettice YL, Smith WA, et al. Buspirone effect on tobacco withdrawal symptoms: a randomized placebo-controlled trial. J Am Board Fam Pract 1992; 5: 1-9

70. Hilleman DE, Mohiuddin SM, Del Core MG, et al. Effect of buspirone on withdrawal symptoms associated with smoking cessation. Arch Intern Med 1992; 152: 350-2

71. Cinciripini PM, Lapitsky L, Seay S, et al. A placebo-controlled evaluation of the effects of buspirone on smoking cessation: differences between high- and low-anxiety smokers. J Clin Psychopharmacol 1995; 15: 182-91

72. Schneider NG, Olmstead R, Steinberg C, et al. Efficacy of buspirone in smoking cessation: a placebo-controlled trial. Clin Pharmacol Ther 1996; 60: 568-75

73. Stolerman IP. Could nicotine antagonists be used in smoking cessation? Br J Addict 1986; 81: 47-53

74. Stolerman IP, Goldfarb T, Fink R, et al. Influencing cigarette smoking with nicotine antagonists. Psychopharmacologia 1973; 28: 247-59

75. Rose JE, Behm FM, Westman EC. Nicotine-mecamylamine treatment for smoking cessation: the role of pre-cessation therapy. Exp Clin Psychopharmacol 1998; 6: 331-43

76. Henningfield JE, Miyasato K, Johnson RE, et al. Rapid physiologic effects of nicotine in humans and selective blockade of behavioral effects by mecamylamine. In: Harris LS, editor. Problems of drug dependence, 1982. Rockville (MD): U.S. Department of Health, Education & Welfare, 1983: 259-65. (NIDA Research Monograph Series No. 43.)
77. Tennant FS, Tarver AL. Withdrawal from nicotine dependence using mecamyalamine: comparison of three-week and six-week dosage schedules. In: Harris LS, editor. Problems of drug dependence, 1984. Proceedings of the 46th Annual Scientific Meeting, the Committee on Problems of Drug Dependence, Inc. Rockville (MD): Department of Health and Human Services & National Institute on Drug Abuse, 1985: 291-7. (NIDA Research Monograph Series No. 55)
78. Eissenberg T, Griffiths RR, Stitzer ML. Mecamylamine does not precipitate withdrawal in cigarette smokers. Psychopharmacology 1996; 127: 328-36
79. Rose JE, Levin ED. Concurrent agonist-antagonist administration for the analysis and treatment of drug dependence. Pharmacol Biochem Behav 1991; 41: 219-26
80. Rose JE, Behm FM, Westman EC. Brand-switching and gender effects in mecamylamine/nicotine smoking cessation treatment. Nicotine Tobacco Res 1999; 1: 286-7
81. Rose JE, Behm FM, Levin ED. Role of nicotine dose and sensory cues in the regulation of smoke intake. Pharmacol Biochem Behav 1993; 44: 891-900
82. Levin ED, Behm F, Carnahan E, et al. Clinical trials using ascorbic acid aerosol to aid smoking cessation. Drug Alcohol Depend 1993; 33: 211-23
83. Westman EC, Behm FM, Rose JE. Airway sensory replacement combined with nicotine replacement for smoking cessation: a randomized, placebo-controlled trial using a citric acid inhaler. Chest 1995; 107: 1358-64
84. Rose JE, Behm FM. Inhalation of vapor from black pepper extract reduces smoking withdrawal symptoms. Drug Alcohol Depend 1994; 34: 225-9
85. Malcolm R, Currey HS, Mitchell MA, et al. Silver acetate gum as a deterrent to smoking. Chest 1986; 90: 107-11
86. Jensen EJ, Schmidt E, Pedersen B, et al. Effect on smoking cessation of silver acetate, nicotine and ordinary chewing gum. Psychopharmacology 1991; 104: 470-4
87. Morrow R, Nepps P, McIntosh M. Silver acetate mouth spray as an aid in smoking cessation: results of a double-blind trial. J Am Board Fam Pract 1993; 6: 353-7
88. Hymowitz N, Eckholdt H. Effects of a 2.5 mg silver acetate lozenge on initial and long-term smoking cessation. Prev Med 1996; 25: 537-46
89. Houdi AA, Pierzchala K, Marson L, et al. Nicotine induced alteration in Tyr-Gly-Gly and metenkephalin in discrete brain nuclei reflects altered enkephalin neuron activity. Peptide 1991; 12: 161-6
90. Malin DH, Lake RL, Carter VA, et al. Naloxone precipitated nicotine abstinence syndrome in the rat. Psychopharmacology 1993; 112: 339-42
91. Krishnan-Sarin S, Rosen MI, O'Malley SS. Naloxone challenge in smokers. Preliminary evidence of an opioid component in nicotine dependence. Arch Gen Psychiatry 1999; 56: 663-8
92. Karras A, Kane JM. Naloxone reduces cigarette smoking. Life Sci 1980; 27: 1541-5
93. Gorelick DA, Rose J, Jarvik ME. Effect of naloxone on cigarette smoking. J Subst Abuse 1989; 1: 153-9
94. Nemeth-Coslett R, Griffiths RR. Naloxone does not affect cigarette smoking. Psychopharmacology 1986; 89 (3): 261-4
95. Sutherland G, Stapleton JA, Russell MAH, et al. Naltrexone, smoking behaviou and cigarette withdrawal. Psychopharmacology 1995; 120: 418-25
96. Wong GY, Wolter TD, Croghan GA, et al. A randomized trial of naltrexone for smoking cessation. Addiction 1999; 94: 1227-37
97. Bourne S. Treatment of cigarette smoking with short-term high-dosage corticotrophin therapy: preliminary communication. J R Soc Med 1985; 78: 649-50
98. McElhaney JL. Repository corticotropin injection as an adjunct to smoking cessation during the initial nicotine withdrawal period: results from a family practice clinic. Clin Ther 1989; 11: 854-61
99. Teng L, Crooks PA, Sonsalla PK, et al. Lobeline and nicotine evoke [$^3$H]overflow from rat striatal slices preloaded with [$^3$H]dopamine: differential inhibition of synaptosomal and vesicular [$^3$H]dopamine uptake. J Pharmacol Exp Ther 1997; 280: 1432-44
100. Damaj MI, Patrick GS, Creasy KR, et al. Pharmacology of lobeline, a nicotinic receptor ligand. J Pharmacol Exp Ther 1997; 282: 410-9
101. Rapp GW, Olen AA. A critical evaluation of a lobeline based smoking deterrent. Am J Med Sci 1955; 9-14
102. Dorsey JL. Control of the tobacco habit. Ann Intern Med 1936; 10: 628-31
103. Kalyuzhnyy VV. The treatment of nicotinism with the aid of lobeline and its influence on vegetative and vascular reactions. J Neural Psychiatry 1968; 68: 1864-70
104. Bartlett WA, Whitehead RW. The effectiveness of meprobamate and lobeline as smoking deterrents. J Lab Clin Med 1957; 50: 278-81
105. Wright IS, Littauer D. Lobeline sulfate: its pharmacology and use in the treatment of the tobacco habit. JAMA 1937; 109: 649-54
106. Tonnesen P, Nørregaard J, Säwe U, et al. Recycling with nicotine patches in smoking cessation. Addiction 1993; 88: 533-9
107. Benowitz NL, Gourlay SG. Cardiovascular toxicity of nicotine: implications for nicotine replacement therapy. J Am Coll Cardiol 1997; 29: 1422-31
108. Joseph AM, Norman SM, Ferry LH, et al. The safety of transdermal nicotine as an aid to smoking cessation in patients with cardiac disease. N Engl J Med 1996; 335: 1792-8
109. Benowitz NL. Nicotine replacement therapy during pregnancy. JAMA 1991; 266: 3174-7

110. Sullivan JP, Donnelly-Roberts D, Briggs CA, et al. ABT-089 [2-methyl-3-(2-(S)-pyrrolidinylmethoxy)pyridine]: I. A potent and selective cholinergic channel modulator with neuroprotective properties. J Pharmacol Exp Ther 1997; 283: 235-46

111. Bencherif M, Lovette ME, Fowler KW, et al. RJR-2403: a nicotinic agonist with CNS selectivity. I. In vitro characterization. J Pharmacol Exp Ther 1996; 279: 1413-21

112. Hieda Y, Keyler DE, Vandevoort JT, et al. Active immunization alters the plasma nicotine concentration in rats. J Pharmacol Exp Ther 1997; 283: 1076-81

113. Keyler DE, Hieda Y, St Peter J, et al. Altered disposition of repeated nicotine doses in rats immunized against nicotine. Nicotine Tobacco Res 1999; 1: 241-9

114. Carrera MRA, Ashley JA, Parsons LH, et al. Suppression of psychoactive effects of cocaine by active immunization. Nature (Lond) 1995; 378: 727-30

115. Fox BS, Kantak KM, Edwards MA, et al. Efficacy of a therapeutic cocaine vaccine in rodent models. Natural Med 1996; 2: 1129-32

---

Correspondence: Dr *Neal L. Benowitz,* Division of Clinical Pharmacology and Experimental Therapeutics, University of California, San Francisco, Box 1220, San Francisco, CA 94143-1220, USA.
E-mail: nbeno@itsa.ucsf.edu

# Smoking Cessation in Individuals with Depression
## Recommendations for Treatment

*Taru Kinnunen*[1,2] and *Beth L. Nordstrom*[1]

1   Harvard School of Dental Medicine, Department of Oral Health Policy and
    Epidemiology, Smoking Research, Boston, Massachusetts, USA
2   University of Jyväskylä, Department of Psychology, Jyväskylä, Finland

## 1. The Link Between Depression and Smoking

Current, historical and subclinical[1] depression have been linked to a high incidence of cigarette smoking and smoking cessation relapse.[1] Also, nondepressed individuals who have some risk factors for depression may experience a major depressive episode while trying to give up cigarettes.[2] One study found that female smokers in family practice settings scored higher on a depression scale than female nonsmokers, and those patients who reported higher cigarette consumption also reported higher levels of depression.[3]

There seem to be two main reasons for this link between depression and nicotine addiction. First, the biological reinforcing effects of nicotine appear to be more important for depressed than for nondepressed smokers. Depressed individuals report smoking more frequently to alleviate negative affect and to provide a substitution for food when they are hungry,[4,5] both of which indicate that depressed individuals obtain more negative reinforcement from smoking than nondepressed individuals. In addition, depressed smokers report smoking more for the stimulant effects than nondepressed smokers, a form of positive reinforcement.[4,5] Anticipation of the relief of a negative state and/or the experience of pleasure may then contribute to the maintenance of nicotine intake.

The second possible reason for the link between nicotine addiction and depression involves withdrawal severity. Nicotine withdrawal, as defined by DSM-IV,[6] can include any of the symptoms outlined in table I. It has been shown that depressed smokers abstaining from smoking experience more severe nicotine withdrawal than nondepressed smokers attempting to quit,[7] which may lead depressed smokers to return to smoking. It is interesting to note that some reports have also shown that women may experience more severe withdrawal syndromes than men.[8] It is possible that the gender difference in withdrawal may merely reflect a higher prevalence of depression among women than men, with no gender difference among non-depressed smokers.

---

1   Subclinical depression is defined as high levels of depressive symptoms, which do not reach the required criteria for a major depressive disorder.

Based on these results and others, cigarette use among depressed smokers may be considered as self-medication.[9] Lerman et al.[5] found that depressed smokers were more likely to report self-medication processes in their reasons for smoking than were nondepressed smokers. Additional support for the self-medication hypothesis was found in a study in which treatment with the transdermal nicotine patch (mean dose of nicotine absorbed per 24 hours of 17.5mg) was used among nonsmok-

**Table I.** Withdrawal symptoms associated with smoking cessation

| |
|---|
| Dysphoria |
| Insomnia |
| Irritability |
| Anxiety |
| Difficulty concentrating |
| Restlessness |
| Decreased heart rate |
| Increased appetite or bodyweight gain |

ers. The study reported that nicotine patches led to an improvement in mood among depressed, but not nondepressed, nonsmokers.[10] Consistent with this are reports from animal models of depression, where nicotine has been observed to have effects similar to those of anti-depressants.[11] If self-medication is the underlying reason for the higher prevalence of smoking among depressed individuals, pharmacological treatments including nicotine replacement and antidepressants seem to be the obvious treatment choices. The efficacy of such treatments is reviewed in sections 2 and 3.

Additional factors influencing the depression-nicotine link include hypotheses that depressed individuals may be more susceptible than nondepressed individuals to becoming smokers and maintaining the habit because of low self-esteem and self-efficacy. Depressed smokers may thus lack the confidence that is required for successful cessation. It may also be that depressed individuals have more general distress (stress, or physical or psychological symptoms) and use cigarettes as a coping mechanism. Giving up smoking then eliminates a coping mechanism and adds more psychological and physical symptoms during the withdrawal phase.[4]

## 2. Nicotine Replacement Therapy

### 2.1 Basics of Nicotine Replacement

Four forms of nicotine replacement are currently available in the USA: nicotine polacrilex gum, transdermal nicotine patch, nicotine nasal spray and nicotine aerosol inhaler. The former two therapies are available over the counter, while the latter two are available only by prescription. In Europe, a sublingual tablet is also available over the counter. The underlying principle of each of the forms is the same: the treatments replace the nicotine usually obtained from cigarettes, minimising withdrawal symptoms and cravings for cigarettes, and consequently making cessation easier. The rate of absorption, adverse effects and compliance with nicotine replacement vary, however, by delivery method.[12] While cigarettes deliver nicotine in the form of repeated, brief and high-concentration doses into the brain, all of the forms of nicotine replacement deliver nicotine more slowly. The nicotine patch has the slowest rate of delivery of any form; thus, though effective in reducing withdrawal symptom severity, some studies,[13] but not all,[14] have found the patch to be less effective than the other forms of nicotine replacement for the elimination of cravings. Nicotine polacrilex gum and inhaler provide somewhat faster delivery, and the nasal spray the fastest delivery of nicotine to the brain, but compliance with these forms of medication is markedly lower than with the patch.[14]

The inhaler and nasal spray, especially, have very poor compliance rates,[14] probably because of the greater likelihood of adverse effects than with the patch or gum.[15,16] In spite of the differences among the various forms of nicotine replacement, however, all have produced similar abstinence rates.[12-17]

## 2.2 Nicotine Polacrilex Gum

The general efficacy of nicotine gum as an aid to smoking cessation is well established.[17] In addition, its effectiveness in depressed smokers has been investigated specifically.[4]

In a community-based sample in Boston, Massachusetts, US, the effectiveness of nicotine gum (with brief behavioural counselling) was tested in a double-blind, placebo-controlled fashion. 32% of the smokers enrolled in the study met the criterion for depression as defined by the Center for Epidemiological Studies Depression Scale (CES-D). Results, which are presented in figure 1, showed that both nicotine gum usage and lower levels of depressive symptoms were associated with quitting success. Relapse was defined as 7 consecutive days or occasions (e.g. consecutive weekends) of smoking;[18] participants who did not meet the criterion for relapse were classified as abstinent. The most successful participants were those who were not depressed and who used nicotine gum (rather than placebo): these individuals had a 1-year abstinence rate of 20.1%. Depressed smokers using nicotine gum were nearly as successful, with a 1-year abstinence rate of 15.1%. Nondepressed participants using placebo gum had 1-year quit rates of only 9.8%. The least successful group was the depressed smokers using placebo gum: their abstinence rates were significantly lower than all the other groups, with only 5.7% able to abstain for the entire 1-year follow-up period.[4]

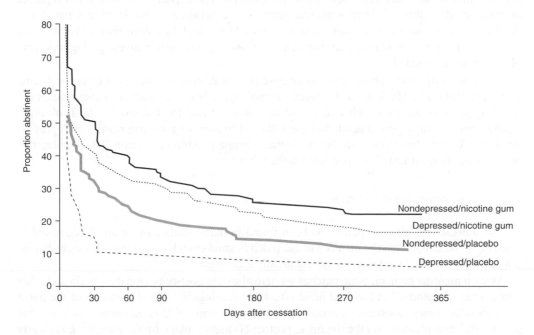

**Fig. 1.** Abstinence rates among nondepressed and depressed smokers (n = 608) using nicotine or placebo gum.[4]

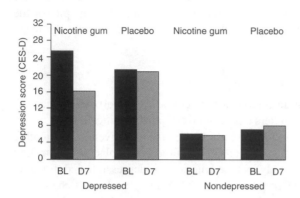

**Fig. 2.** Changes in depressive symptoms from baseline (BL) to day 7 (D7) post-cessation in 278 smokers treated with nicotine or placebo gum. **CES-D** = Center for Epidemiological Studies Depression Scale.

With regard to depressive symptoms, at day 7, day 30, month 2 and month 3, consistent significant findings emerged. Among depressed smokers using nicotine gum, depression scores decreased significantly from baseline to each post-cessation assessment. In contrast, no statistically significant changes in depression scores were observed among the other treatment groups (see fig. 2 for day 7 results).[4]

Other studies have shown that nicotine gum alleviates post-cessation dysphoria.[19] In general, nicotine gum appears to be most effective when combined with behavioural counselling,[20] and seems to suppress several withdrawal symptoms, but not cravings.[13]

The adverse effects of nicotine gum are usually minimal; they can include hiccups, jaw discomfort, mild nausea and flatulence. Typically, the adverse effects can be eliminated by proper chewing technique. One drawback to nicotine gum, however, is that compliance can be problematic. In the study described above, for example, participants used a mean of 8 pieces of gum per day, although they were instructed to use between 9 and 15 pieces per day.[4] Preliminary evidence suggests that the sublingual tablet, which functions much like the gum, may lead to better compliance than the gum.[21,22] Additional studies investigating this form of treatment are needed.

Questions still remain about appropriate dose and duration of treatment. For example, is 2mg gum sufficient for highly dependent, depressed smokers, or is it necessary for these smokers to use 4mg gum, or an even higher dose? Also, it may be that the typical 2-month nicotine replacement therapy period needs to be lengthened to achieve adequate results in depressed smokers. Reports from some studies with the nicotine patch (see section 2.3) support this recommendation for heavily dependent smokers.[23]

## 2.3 Transdermal Nicotine Patch

The transdermal nicotine patch has been found in many studies to be an effective aid in smoking cessation,[24] but the efficacy of the patch in smokers who are depressed at the beginning of treatment has not yet been systematically examined.

As with nicotine gum, nicotine patches seem to alleviate post-cessation dysphoria and other withdrawal symptoms, but have minimal effects on cravings.[25] Adverse effects of the patch are generally minor, consisting primarily of skin irritations.[26] One advantage of using the patch is that compliance with the treatment protocol is higher than with the gum;[13] it is clearly more convenient to apply a patch once each day than to chew several pieces of gum every day.

It has been suggested that higher degrees of nicotine replacement are beneficial for depressed[4] and highly dependent smokers. Delivering higher doses may be easier with patches than with gum. Results from studies using higher dose patches (42mg of nicotine delivered per 24 hours) have been mixed: one study found a short term increase in abstinence rates for heavily dependent smokers,[27] but this effect was not found by other researchers.[28] Several investigations are currently in progress investigating the optimal dosage level, treatment duration, and tapering of the dose.

## 2.4 Nicotine Nasal Spray and Nicotine Inhaler

Similarly to nicotine gum and transdermal patch, the nicotine nasal spray and inhaler have been found to increase abstinence rates among the general population of smokers, but we found no reports assessing these treatments among depressed smokers.[15,16,29,30] The nasal spray was found to be particularly effective for heavily dependent smokers.[15]

Both the nasal spray and the inhaler relieve not only withdrawal symptoms, but also, unlike the nicotine gum or patch, cigarette cravings.[15,29] Undesirable adverse effects, however, are very common with both the spray and the inhaler. Adverse effects of the nicotine inhaler include irritation in the nose and throat, watering eyes and coughing; one or more of these symptoms was experienced by almost all participants.[15,16,29,30] The inhaler commonly causes coughing and throat or mouth irritation, and occasionally has been found to cause nausea, indigestion and headache.[16,29,31]

## 2.5 Combination Treatment with Nicotine Replacement Therapies

In an attempt to improve smoking cessation outcomes, some studies[32-36] have used nicotine replacement products in combination. In combination therapy, nicotine replacement products may be used concurrently, sequentially, or both. Treatments given concurrently (i.e. both forms of treatment beginning and ending at the same time) have included the patch and gum[32-34] and the patch plus inhaler.[35] Sequential combination treatments often involve a regimen in which initially only the patch is given, but after patch therapy ends, the gum, inhaler, tablet or nasal spray may be used as needed for long periods for relapse prevention. A mix of concurrent and sequential nicotine replacement has been used, for example, in a study in which initially the patch and nasal spray were used concurrently, followed by a period in which only the nasal spray was continued.[36] All the published studies suggest that combination nicotine replacement therapy leads to better success than a single modality.[32-36]

Combining nicotine replacement therapies has been suggested as a particularly desirable approach in depressed smokers, based on different pharmacokinetic and biological reinforcing effects of the different forms of nicotine replacement therapy. For example, a study that combined the nicotine patch (21mg per 16 hours) with 2mg nicotine gum found that post-cessation dysphoric mood ratings were lower than precessation ratings; however, this study did not assess the effects separately for depressed and nondepressed smokers.[32]

Combination treatment is also an important approach for ensuring that an adequate therapeutic dose of nicotine is delivered. To achieve a desirable nicotine replacement delivery system and degree of nicotine replacement (possibly 100% of the precessation nicotine intake), therapeutic drug monitoring may be needed. Concentrations of nicotine and its metabolite, cotinine, can be measured in the blood, and cotinine can also be measured in saliva and urine.

In fact, at least two US-based biochemical companies are developing 'quick and easy' cotinine urine dipstick tests, which could perhaps be used for simple individualisation of nicotine replacement therapy, assuring an adequate replacement level while avoiding overdosage.

As discussed below, mixed-modality combination therapies, such as nicotine patch plus bupropion[37] or nicotine nasal inhaler and fluoxetine,[38] have also been examined, with encouraging results. Other agents such as nortriptyline and doxepin should also be tested in combination with nicotine replacement.

### 2.6 Additional Issues

Complicating the picture of smoking cessation and nicotine replacement are possible gender differences. Several research findings suggest that quitting smoking is more difficult for women than men,[39] and that nicotine replacement may not be as effective in alleviating withdrawal symptoms for women as for men.[40] However, other studies have not found these differences (e.g. Fiore et al.[41]). The reasons why smoking cessation may be more difficult for women are not clear, but several explanations have been suggested. Demographic background and smoking history may be different for women than for men, and the benefits of smoking that women may perceive may be difficult to replace (e.g. mood management and bodyweight control). Finally, other critical variables associated with quitting success (e.g. self-efficacy, social support, negative affect) may differ by gender.[39] Since depression is more prevalent among women, the above factors should be taken into account in treatment planning.

## 3. Non-Nicotine Pharmacological Therapies

### 3.1 Selective Serotonin Reuptake Inhibitors

Given the efficacy of selective serotonin (5-hydroxytryptamine; 5-HT) reuptake inhibitors (SSRIs) in the treatment of depression *per se*, treating depressed smokers with these drugs appears to be a logical choice. However, the studies conducted to date have not found SSRIs to be particularly effective in enhancing abstinence rates. Many studies using SSRIs have not reported smoking abstinence rates, but rather have concentrated on examining the effects on post-cessation withdrawal symptoms. One study that did discuss the effects of SSRIs on abstinence rates used zimeldine (zimelidine) [200 mg/day] among heavy drinkers attempting to quit smoking, but observed no benefit from the drug, compared with placebo, on abstinence rates.[42]

One study[43] found that fluoxetine 20mg twice daily, starting 3 weeks prior to quitting (during the first week of treatment the drug dosage was 20 mg/day), reduced post-cessation depression, anger and tension, compared with placebo. Borrelli et al.[44] examined fluoxetine 30 and 60 mg/day (treatment was started 2 weeks prior to quit day) and placebo among participants who were not clinically depressed at the onset of the study. 7% of the participants, however, developed major depressive disorder during the smoking cessation treatment. None of these study participants was receiving fluoxetine 60 mg/day, suggesting that this dosage of fluoxetine may be a prophylactic to the onset of depression.

Another study[45] using fluoxetine 30 and 60 mg/day, starting 2 weeks prior to the quit day, found that the medication improved abstinence rates for 3 months post-cessation only among smokers with high baseline depression scores who complied with the treatment protocol. The 60mg/day dosage group was not examined separately from the 30mg/day group, so any effect of dose is unknown. Similar results were found in a study[38] in which smokers were given

both nicotine inhalers and fluoxetine 20 mg/day, or nicotine inhalers and placebo. Fluoxetine again increased abstinence rates only for those who had high baseline depression scores. In this study, the effect of fluoxetine was not limited to those who complied with the treatment regimen, and it persisted through a 1-year follow-up. It is thus possible that 20 mg/day of fluoxetine is sufficient for smoking cessation in depressed individuals if it is accompanied by another form of pharmacotherapy such as nicotine replacement.

If SSRIs are used in depressed smokers, treatment should probably begin earlier than in reported studies (4 to 8 weeks prior to the quit date) to allow the onset of antidepressant effect prior to initiating the quit attempt. Also, when used as the sole pharmacological treatment, the dose may have to be higher than 20 mg/day, possibly as high as 60 mg/day, to achieve the desired results. In addition to the study by Borrelli et al.,[44] anecdotal clinical evidence suggests that the higher dosages used for the treatment of obsessive-compulsive disorder may be helpful for smokers. However, the obvious concern with the use of high dosages of SSRIs is heightened likelihood of adverse effects, such as insomnia, headaches, nausea and disturbed sexual function.[46]

Although fluoxetine appears to be a promising aid for smoking cessation in depressed smokers, more placebo-controlled studies investigating its effects on long term abstinence, withdrawal and cravings are still needed. Furthermore, studies using other SSRIs such as sertraline and SSRIs in combination with nicotine replacement therapy should be conducted.

## 3.2 Amfebutamone (Bupropion)

Immediate-release (300 mg/day for 12 weeks) and sustained-release (100, 150 and 300 mg/day for 7 weeks, beginning at 1 week precessation) amfebutamone has been shown to increase abstinence rates and to decrease the severity of withdrawal symptoms among a non-depressed population of smokers.[37,47,48] Sustained-release amfebutamone has also been found to improve cessation rates among smokers with a history of major depressive disorder but not of alcoholism.[49] Sustained-release amfebutamone has been approved by the US Food and Drug Administration as an aid to smoking cessation. However, the effectiveness of this form of therapy for smokers with current depression has not been examined adequately.

The two most comprehensive studies to date found that sustained-released amfebutamone did not influence post-cessation depressive symptoms among individuals who were not depressed at the beginning of cessation.[47,48] This is similar to our findings,[4] where nicotine gum reduced depressive symptoms only among patients who had high levels of depressive symptoms at the beginning of the cessation period.

Amfebutamone was found to reduce post-cessation bodyweight gain,[45] which may make it advantageous for those who are concerned about bodyweight gain or for whom bodyweight issues are related to depressive symptoms.[50] Findings have been inconsistent regarding the effect of amfebutamone on other withdrawal symptoms. One study found no effect,[47] whereas another found amfebutamone to significantly reduce withdrawal.[37] In another study,[51] the 300 mg/day dose led to a decrease in depression, irritability and difficulty concentrating in 3-day abstainers from smoking. On the whole, however, the effect of amfebutamone on withdrawal and cravings appears to be relatively small.[51]

Adverse effects associated with treatment were primarily insomnia and dry mouth, although it is important to note that 3 of 156 participants receiving amfebutamone 300 mg/day had

serious adverse reactions (i.e. extreme irritability and anxiety, an allergic reaction, and cardiac arrest).[46]

Hurt et al.[48] recommended 300 mg/day (150mg twice a day) as the target dosage for most patients. They used a 7-week treatment period, modelled on studies of nicotine replacement therapy, but recognised that longer treatment may be more desirable, particularly since antidepressants are commonly used for longer durations in the treatment of depression and chronic pain without major risk for abuse. Jorenby et al.[37] obtained good results with a 9-week treatment period.

A recent study has examined amfebutamone in combination with nicotine patches, and found this treatment to be both well tolerated and effective, although not significantly more effective than amfebutamone alone.[37] The specific effects of this combination among depressed smokers have yet to be determined.

### 3.3 Nortriptyline

Nortriptyline hydrochloride, a tricyclic antidepressant, has been investigated in two placebo-controlled, double-blind studies in smokers with and without a history of major depressive disorder.[52,53] Prochazka et al.[52] administered nortriptyline dosages of 25 mg/day, titrated to 75 mg/day, beginning 10 days before the quit day. Hall et al.[53] used similar dosages, but titrated to a maximum of 100 mg/day, and began treatment 4 weeks before the quit day. Both studies found that nortriptyline significantly improved abstinence rates at 6 months and 1 year, respectively, and that the effect of nortriptyline was the same for participants with and without a history of major depressive disorder. Prochazka et al.[52] found the medication to reduce several withdrawal symptoms, including anxiety/tension, anger/irritability, difficulty concentrating, restlessness and impatience. In contrast, Hall et al.[53] found no effect on total withdrawal score, although nortriptyline did decrease negative affect. Although these results are promising, nortriptyline has one major drawback: adverse effects are very common, especially dry mouth, lightheadedness and drowsiness.[52,53] Nevertheless, the effectiveness of this medication for smokers with a history of major depression suggests that additional studies using nortriptyline as an aid to smoking cessation in individuals with current depression are warranted.

### 3.4 Doxepin

The efficacy of doxepin, in dosages of 150 mg/day, as an aid to smoking cessation has been investigated in two preliminary studies. The first[54,55] found that smokers who used doxepin were more likely to abstain from smoking during a quit attempt than individuals using a placebo. The second[56] showed that doxepin led to a significant reduction in cigarette cravings during abstinence. Neither of the studies investigated the effects of doxepin in depressed smokers. Although no definite conclusions can be drawn from these two pilot studies, it is evident that doxepin has the potential to be a possible smoking cessation treatment for individuals with depression.

### 3.5 Clonidine

Although results from investigations of clonidine have been somewhat inconsistent, the drug appears to have some promise as a smoking cessation treatment, particularly for

reducing withdrawal symptoms.[57,58] However, the optimal dose and efficacy among depressed smokers have yet to be determined. Clonidine (0.05mg 4 times daily) was effective in inducing cessation and reducing cravings in heavily dependent smokers, when treatment was started 1 week prior to quitting.[57] In another study, in which a higher dosage was used (0.20mg twice daily), no gain in abstinence rates or withdrawal control was found.[59] Transdermal clonidine (0.10 mg/day), however, was found to reduce the severity of withdrawal symptoms in another study.[58]

A meta-analysis of studies with long term cessation outcomes found that clonidine was effective in promoting abstinence, especially for women.[60] Glassman et al.[61] found clonidine to be an effective smoking cessation treatment for women with a history of recurrent depression, and particularly for those who were also highly dependent on nicotine. Unfortunately, clonidine has a high rate of adverse effects, including sedation, dry mouth and dizziness.[60]

Since nicotine gum and patches typically do not reduce post-cessation cravings, clonidine may thus be a promising treatment for depressed smokers, since many such individuals attempting to quit report particularly intense cravings.[62] Clonidine and doxepin should be tested in controlled studies in combination with nicotine replacement.

## 4. Cognitive-Behavioural Therapy

Providing counselling to depressed smokers attempting to quit may help to increase self-esteem and self-efficacy, which may empower a depressed smoker to quit, or at least increase the likelihood of his or her adhering to the smoking cessation regimen.[2] Cognitive-behavioural therapy is often used as an adjunct to pharmacological treatments.[35,45,47]

There is some evidence suggesting that depressed smokers may benefit from cognitive-behavioural counselling beyond the basic smoking cessation counselling. Hall and colleagues[45,52,53] investigated the efficacy of a cognitive-behavioural mood management intervention that focused on helping smokers to develop skills that would allow them to manage the affective distress that often occurs with smoking cessation. Before the quit day, smokers monitored their smoking and their moods and discussed the relationships between the two parameters. After cessation, participants evaluated their current thought patterns about smoking and practiced alternative ways to deal with relapse-related thoughts (e.g. thought stopping, rational-emotive techniques). The intervention also focused on increasing the frequency of pleasant activities, improving social support and learning relaxation techniques.

Two studies that Hall et al. carried out found mood management intervention in combination with nicotine gum[63] and in combination with nortriptyline[53] to improve cessation rates for smokers with a history of depression. However, another study[64] found that this treatment approach was statistically not significantly more effective than an equal therapeutic contact (health education) control condition. The lack of significance must be regarded with caution, however, because the statistical power was low. In the second study, among participants with a history of major depression, 33% of patients in the mood management group, but only 22% of those in the control group, were abstinent at 1 year post-cessation.[64] This intervention clearly deserves further research in depressed smokers.

The literature on depression has for decades outlined the importance of physical exercise as a mood management technique. Although little research has been conducted to date investigating the effectiveness of exercise as an aid to smoking cessation, some small trials have yielded encouraging results.[65, 66] For depressed smokers, the importance of proper diet, exercise, adequate rest and other healthy behaviours should be emphasised and integrated into all smoking cessation programmes or advice regimens.[2]

## 5. Additional Considerations for Treatment

Concerns about bodyweight gain may contribute to quitting difficulties, particularly among female smokers (who are the individuals most likely to be vulnerable to depression). Treatments such as nicotine gum and amfebutamone, either alone or in combination, that address both depression and bodyweight gain are recommended for all female smokers. Also, preliminary results from an ongoing trial at the University of Pittsburgh in the US suggest that cognitive-behavioural treatment may be helpful for women with bodyweight concerns.[67]

Another special subgroup to be considered is pregnant smokers. The advantages of cessation during pregnancy are obvious and the risk for depression higher at this time than at others,[68,69] but clinical trials establishing the safety and efficacy of pharmacological interventions for smoking cessation among pregnant smokers are lacking. However, there are recent studies (e.g. Schou[70]) which suggest that antidepressants such as nortriptyline and SSRIs may be well tolerated during pregnancy. Furthermore, nicotine replacement therapies, when used appropriately, do not yield any more nicotine per day than a pack of cigarettes, and hence are less likely to endanger pregnant women and their fetuses than smoking.

## 6. Recommendations for Treatment

### 6.1 Screening for Depression

Conducting structured clinical interviews to determine depressive status – although desirable – is usually not feasible in primary care settings. We have found the CES-D[71] to be a reliable, valid and useful self-report measure of current depression in smokers. It has 20 items that are very simple to score. Scores over 15 (from a range of 0 to 60) are considered to reflect depression. Additional questions about past episodes and symptoms, and family history of depression, as well as possible postpartum or post-cessation depression, would be helpful in optimal treatment planning. Other common assessment criteria for depression, such as the Hamilton Depression Rating Scale and the Montgomery-Åsberg Depression Rating Scale, are also useful.

### 6.2 Screening for Nicotine Dependency

In determining the optimal smoking cessation treatment for a given individual, it is important to assess the smoker's nicotine dependency level. A variety of instruments for measuring nicotine dependency exist. The simplest, and hence easiest to administer, and most reliable and valid dependency scale is the Heaviness of Smoking Index (HSI).[72] The HSI consists of two items: (i) the number of cigarettes smoked per day; and (ii) the time to first cigarette upon waking in the morning. Each item is rated on a 0 to 3 scale, and responses are summed to create a scale ranging from 0 to 6. A score of between 0 and 3 is considered to reflect low dependency, while a score of 4 to 6 represents high dependency. Administration of this simple scale to depressed smokers provides valuable guidance in deciding upon treatment methods.

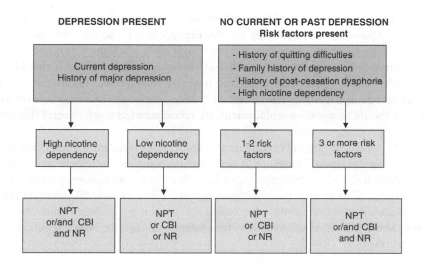

**Fig. 3.** Guidelines for choosing a treatment regimen to assist depressed (left-hand section) or at-risk (right-hand section) smokers quit smoking. **CBI** = cognitive-behavioural intervention; **NPT** = non-nicotine pharmacological treatment; **NR** = nicotine replacement (single or combination treatment).

## 6.3 Choice of Treatment Modality

Guidelines for treatment decision-making are presented in figure 3. It should be noted that many of the treatments suggested have yet to be tested in randomised controlled studies with depressed smokers. During the screening process, the healthcare provider should assess whether: (i) the patient is depressed (current or history of depression); and (ii) there are additional risk factors for the development of depression during a smoking cessation attempt. These risk factors include, but are not limited to:

- a history of quitting difficulties (several unsuccessful attempts and/or longest previous quit attempt lasting only days or weeks rather than months)
- a history of post-cessation dysphoria (patient reports having felt sad or depressed during a previous quit attempt)
- a family history of depression
- a high level of nicotine dependency.

In individuals in whom depression is present and there is a high level of nicotine dependence, a combination of therapies addressing the depression [non-nicotine pharmacological treatment (NPT) or cognitive-behavioural therapy] and nicotine dependence (replacement therapy) is recommended. Emphasis should be placed on providing treatment for the depression for a sufficient length of time, and on achieving adequate levels of nicotine replacement (high-dose patch or a combination of nicotine replacement therapies). In contrast, a single treatment modality may be sufficient for those who are not highly dependent, but who have depressive symptoms. The decision as to which treatment to use should be based on the patient's medical, psychiatric and smoking history.

A single modality of treatment may also be adequate in individuals who are not depressed and do not have a history of depression, but in whom one or two other risk factors for depression exist. Treatment should be based on the specific risk factors and smoking history. For example, in patients who are highly nicotine dependent but who have no other risk factors, nicotine replacement therapy is indicated. However, if there is a history of post-cessation dysphoria, cognitive-behavioural therapy or NPT might be the best approach. It should be kept in mind that individualising and increasing the intensity (dosage and additional modality) of therapy may be indicated if difficulties surface early during cessation. Two modalities of treatment, one of which should be nicotine replacement, are recommended when several risk factors for depression are present.

In general, it must be remembered that most smoking cessation relapses occur within the first 2 weeks post-cessation. Therefore, if possible, in-person and/or telephone follow-up visits should be scheduled, and modifications and individualisation of therapy performed if withdrawal, cravings, slips or adverse effects so suggest. Furthermore, all interventions should include advice/information about the basics of smoking cessation and other healthy behaviours. Many pamphlets are available, for example, through the National Cancer Institute in the US (www.nih.gov).

## 7. Conclusion

Depression remains one of the main impediments to successful smoking cessation. Some treatment options have been outlined here, but additional research is badly needed, in particular in the area of combining nicotine replacement with other treatment modalities. Efforts should be made to tailor the form or forms of therapy provided to the needs, preferences and history of the individual smoker. If the first treatment used with a given smoker leads to poor compliance, unacceptable adverse effects or poor results, different forms of therapy should be tried until a successful outcome is obtained. Considering that depressed smokers tend to smoke more cigarettes per day and have, on average, smoked more packs during their lifetimes, and thus are at high risk for smoking-related illnesses, additional investigations into the depression-smoking link are warranted.

### Acknowledgements

Preparation of this chapter was supported in part by US Public Service grants NCI-CA72849 and NIDA-DA12503 from the National Institutes of Health. The authors would like to thank Lauri Henning for her contributions to the chapter.

### References
1. Anda RF, Williamson DF, Escobedo LG. Depression and the dynamics of smoking: a national perspective. JAMA 1990; 264: 1541-5
2. Borrelli B, Bock B, King T, et al. The impact of depression on smoking cessation in women. Am J Prev Med 1996; 12 (5): 378-84
3. Tamburrino MB, Lynch DJ, Nagel RW, et al. Screening women in family practice settings: association between depression and smoking cigarettes. Fam Pract Res J 1994; 14 (4): 333-7
4. Kinnunen T, Doherty K, Militello FS, et al. Depression and smoking cessation: characteristics of depressed smokers and effects of nicotine replacement. J Consult Clin Psychol 1996; 64: 791-8
5. Lerman C, Audrain J, Orleans CT, et al. Investigation of mechanisms linking depressed mood to nicotine dependence. Addict Behav 1996; 21: 9-19
6. American Psychiatric Association. Diagnostic and statistical manual of mental disorder. 4th ed. Washington, DC: American Psychiatric Association, 1994
7. Madden PAF, Bucholz, KK, Dinwiddle SH, et al. Nicotine withdrawal in women. Addiction 1997; 92 (7): 889-902
8. Kinnunen T, Nordstrom BL, Utman CH, et al. Gender differences in tobacco use and withdrawal [abstract]. Pharmacol Biochem Behav 1998; 61: 152
9. Hughes JR. Clonidine, depression, and smoking cessation. JAMA 1988; 259 (19): 2901-2

10. Salin-Pascual RJ, de la Fuente JR, Galicia-Polo L, et al. Effects of transdermal nicotine on mood and sleep in non-smoking major depressed patients. Psychopharmacology 1995; 121: 476-9
11. Tizabi Y, Overstreet DH, Rezvani AH, et al. Antidepressant effects of nicotine in an animal model of depression. Psychopharmacology 1999; 142: 193-9
12. Sachs DPL, Fagerström KO. Medical management of tobacco dependence-II: Practical office considerations. Curr Pulmonol 1995; 16: 239-49
13. Benowitz NL. Nicotine replacement therapy: What has been accomplished - Can we do better? Drugs, 1993; 45: 157-70
14. Hajek P, West R, Foulds J, et al. Randomized comparative trial of nicotine polacrilex, a transdermal patch, nasal spray, and an inhaler. Arch Intern Med 1999; 159: 2033-8
15. Sutherland G, Stapleton JA, Russell MA, et al. Randomised controlled trial of nasal nicotine spray in smoking cessation. Lancet 1992; 340: 324-9
16. Schneider NG, Olmstead R, Nilsson F, et al. Efficacy of a nicotine inhaler in smoking cessation: A double-blind, placebo-controlled trial. Addiction 1996; 91: 1293-306
17. Cepeda-Benito A. Meta-analytical review of the efficacy of nicotine chewing gum in smoking treatment programs. J Consult Clin Psychol 1993; 61: 822-30
18. Ossip-Klein DJ, Bigelow G, Parker SR, et al. Classification and assessment of smoking behavior. Health Psychol 1986; 5 Suppl.: 3-11
19. West RJ, Jarvis MJ, Russel MAH, et al. Effect of nicotine replacement on the cigarette withdrawal syndrome. Br J Addiction 1984; 79: 215-9
20. Hughes JR. Pharmacotherapy for smoking cessation: Unvalidated assumptions, anomalies, and suggestions for future research. J Consult Clin Psychol 1993, 61. 751-60
21. Fägerstrom KO, Tejding R, Westin A, et al. Aiding reduction of smoking with nicotine replacement medications: hope for the recalcitrant smoker? Tobacco Control 1997; 6: 311-6
22. Glover ED, Glover PN, Franzon M, et al. A nicotine sublingual tablet for smoking cessation: 12-month data. Proceedings of the Fifth Annual Meeting of the Society for Research on Nicotine and Tobacco, San Diego, CA, March 1999
23. Sachs DPL. Use and efficacy of nicotine patches. J Smok Related Dis 1994; 5 Suppl 1: 183-93
24. Law M, Tang JL. An analysis of the effectiveness of interventions intended to help people stop smoking. Arch Intern Med 1995; 155: 1933-41
25. Westman EC, Levin ED, Rose JE. The nicotine patch in smoking cessation. Arch Intern Med 1993; 153: 1917-23
26. Hurt RD, Dale LC, Fredrickson PA, et al. Nicotine patch therapy for smoking cessation combined with physician advice and nurse follow-up. JAMA 1994; 271: 595-600
27. Dale LC, Hurt RD, Offord KP, et al. High-dose patch therapy: Percentage replacement and smoking cessation. JAMA 1995; 274: 1353-8
28. Jorenby DE, Smith SS, Fiore MC, et al. Varying nicotine patch dose and type of smoking cessation counseling. JAMA 1995; 274: 1347-52
29. Hjalmarson A, Nilsson F, Sjöström L, et al. The nicotine inhaler in smoking cessation. Arch Intern Med 1997; 157: 1721-8
30. Leischow SJ, Nilsson F, Franzon M, et al. Efficacy of the nicotine inhaler as an adjunct to smoking cessation. Am J Health Behavior 1996; 20: 364-71
31. Tonnesen P, Norregaard J, Mikkelsen K, et al. A double-blind trial of a nicotine inhaler for smoking cessation. JAMA 1993; 269: 1268-71
32. Fagerstrom KO, Schneider NG, Lunell E. Effectiveness of nicotine patch and nicotine gum as individual versus combined treatments for tobacco withdrawal symptoms. Psychopharmacology (Berl.) 1993; 111: 271-77
33. Kornitzer M, Boutsen M, Dramaix M, et al. Combined use of nicotine patch and gum in smoking cessation: a placebo-controlled clinical trial. Prev Med 1995; 24: 41-7
34. Puska P, Korhonen HJ, Vartiainen E, et al. Combined use of nicotine patch and gum compared with gum alone in smoking cessation: A clinical trial in North Karelia. Tobacco Control 1995; 4: 231-5
35. Bohadana AB, Nilsson F, Martinet Y. Nicotine inhaler and nicotine patch: A combination therapy for smoking cessation. Nicotine Tobacco Research 1999; 1: 189
36. Blöndal T, Gudmundsson LJ, Olafsdottir I, et al. Nicotine nasal spray with nicotine patch for smoking cessation: randomised trial with a six-year follow up. BMJ 1999; 318: 285-9
37. Jorenby DE, Leischow SJ, Nides MA, et al. A controlled trial of sustained-release bupropion, a nicotine patch, or both for smoking cessation. N Engl J Med 1999; 340: 685-91
38. Blöndal T, Gudmundsson LJ, Tomasson K, et al. The effects of fluoxetine combined with nicotine inhalers in smoking cessation - a randomized trial. Addiction 1999; 94: 1007-15
39. Perkins KA. Sex differences in nicotine versus nonnicotine reinforcement as determinants of tobacco smoking. Exp Clin Psychopharmacol 1996; 4: 166-77
40. Hatsukami D, Skoog K, Allen S, et al. Gender and the effects of different doses of nicotine gum on tobacco withdrawal symptoms. Exp Clin Psychopharmacol 1995; 3: 163-73
41. Fiore MC, Novotny TE, Pierce JP, et al. Methods used to quit smoking in the United States: Do cessation programs help? JAMA 1990; 263: 2760-5
42. Sellers EM, Naranjo CA, Kadlec K. Do serotonin uptake inhibitors decrease smoking? Observations in a group of heavy drinkers. J Clin Psychopharmacol 1987; 7: 417-20
43. Dalack GW, Glassman AH, Rivelli S, et al. Mood, major depression, and fluoxetine response in cigarette smokers. Am J Psychiatry 1995; 152: 398-403

44. Borrelli B, Niaura R, Keuthen NJ, et al. Development of major depressive disorder during smoking-cessation treatment. J Clin Psychiatry 1996; 57: 534-38

45. Hitsman B, Pingitore R, Spring B, et al. Antidepressant pharmacotherapy helps some cigarette smokers more than others. J Consult Clin Psychol 1999; 67: 547-54

46. Maxmen JS, Ward NG. Psychotropic drugs fast facts. W.W. Norton & Company, New York; 1995

47. Ferry, LH; Burchette, RJ. Efficacy of bupropion for smoking cessation in non-depressed smokers. J Addict Dis 1994; 13: 249

48. Hurt RD, Sachs DP, Glover ED, et al. A comparison of sustained-released bupropion and placebo for smoking cessation. New Engl J Med 1997; 337: 1195-202

49. Hayford KE, Patten CA, Rummans TA, et al. Efficacy of bupropion for smoking cessation in smokers with a former history of major depression or alcoholism. Br J Psychiatry 1999; 174: 173-8

50. Lief HI. Bupropion treatment of depression to assist smoking cessation. Am J Psychiatry 1996; 153: 442

51. Shiffman S, Johnston JA, Khayrallah M, et al. The effect of bupropion on nicotine craving and withdrawal. Psychopharmacology 2000; 148: 33-40

52. Prochazka AV, Weaver MJ, Keller RT, et al. A randomized trial of nortiptyline for smoking cessation. Arch Intern Med 1998; 158: 2035-9

53. Hall SM, Reus VI, Muñoz RF, et al. Nortriptyline and cognitive-behavioral therapy in the treatment of cigarette smoking. Arch Gen Psychiatry 1998; 55: 683-90

54. Edwards NB, Murphy JK, Downs AD, et al. Doxepin as an adjunct to smoking cessation: A double-blind pilot study. Am J Psychiatry 1989; 146: 373-6

55. Edwards NP, Simmons RC, Rosenthal TL, et al. Doxepin in the treatment of nicotine withdrawal. Psychosomatics 1988; 29: 203-6

56. Murphy JK, Edwards NB, et al. Effects of doxepin on withdrawal symptoms in smoking cessation. Am J Psychiatry 1990; 147: 1353-7

57. Glassman AH, Steiner F, Walsh BT, et al. Heavy smokers, smoking cessation, and clonidine. JAMA 1988; 259: 2863-6

58. Prochazka AV, Petty TL, Nett L, et al. Transdermal clonidine reduced some withdrawal symptoms but did not increase smoking cessation. Arch Intern Med 1992;52: 2065-9

59. Franks P, Harp J, Bell B. Randomized, controlled trial of clonidine for smoking cessation in a primary care setting. JAMA 1989; 262: 3011-3

60. Gourlay SG, Benowitz NL. Is clonidine an effective smoking cessation therapy? Drugs 1995; 50:197-207

61. Glassman AH, Lirio SC, Gregory WD, et al. Smoking cessation, clonidine, and vulnerability to nicotine among dependent smokers. Clin Pharmacol Ther 1993; 54: 670-9

62. Berlin I, Spreux-Varoquaux O, Said S, et al. Effects of past history of major depression on smoking characteristics, monoamine oxidase-A and B and withdrawal symptoms in dependent smokers. Drug Alcohol Depend 1997; 45: 31-37.

63. Hall SM, Munoz RF, Reus VI. Cognitive-behavioral intervention increases abstinence rates for depressive-history smokers. J Consul Clin Psychol 1994; 62: 141-6

64. Hall SM, Munoz RF, Reus VI, et al. Mood management and nicotine gum in smoking treatment: A therapeutic contact and placebo-controlled study. J Consult Clin Psychol 1996; 64: 1003-9

65. Marcus BH, Albrecht AE, Niaura RS, et al. Usefulness of physical exercise for maintaining smoking cessation in women. Am J Cardiol 1991; 68: 406-7

66. Marcus BH, Albrecht AE, Niaura RS, et al. Exercise enhances the maintenance of smoking cessation in women. Addictive Behaviors 1995; 20: 87-92

67. Perkins KA, Levine M, Marcus M, et al. Behavioral weight control vs. cognitive therapy for weight concerns as adjunct treatment for smoking cessation in women. Ann Behavior Med 1998; 20: PA 21E

68. Murata A, Nadaoka T, Morioka Y, et al. Prevalence and background factors of maternity blues. Gynecol Obstet Invest 1998; 46: 99-104

69. Cameron RP, Grabill CM, Hobfoll SE, et al. Weight, self-esteem, ethnicity, and depressive symptomatology during pregnancy among inner-city women. Health Psychol 1996; 15: 293-7

70. Schou M. Treating recurrent affective disorders during and after pregnancy. What can be taken safely? Drug Saf 1998; 18: 143-52

71. Radloff, LS. The CES-D scale: A self-report depression scale from research in the general population. Appl Psychol Measure 1977; 1: 385-401

72. Heatherton TF, Kozlowski LT, Frecker RC, et al. Measuring the heaviness of smoking: using self-reported time to the first cigarette of the day and number of cigarettes smoked per day. Br J Addict 1989; 84: 791-9

Correspondence: *Taru Kinnunen*, PhD, Harvard School of Dental Medicine, Department of Oral Health Policy and Epidemiology, Smoking Cessation Research, 44 Bromfield Street, Suite 205, Boston, MA 02108, USA.
E-mail: taru_kinnunen@hms.harvard.edu

# Nicotine Replacement Therapy in Patients with Coronary Heart Disease
## Recommendations for Effective Use

*Charlotta Pisinger, Poul Wennike* and *Philip Tønnesen*

Gentofte University Hospital, Niels Andersensvej, Hellerup, Denmark

## 1. General Aspects

### 1.1 Cigarette Smoking

Smoking is the most important preventable cause of morbidity and mortality from cardio-vascular disease.[1,2] Cigarette smoke contains nicotine, carbon monoxide (CO), oxidant gases, polycyclic aromatic hydrocarbons and tar. In fact, it comprises more than 4000 compounds, of which several are potentially cardiotoxic. Cigarette smoke promotes atherosclerosis, and is associated with an increased risk of sudden death, myocardial infarction and unstable angina.[3]

Cigarette smoke increases myocardial work, and thereby oxygen demand, by increasing blood pressure, heart rate (HR) and cardiac output. Also, coronary blood flow is reduced by coronary vasoconstriction and enhanced thrombosis.[1]

The CO in cigarette smoke binds to haemoglobin thereby reducing the oxygen supply to the myocardium.[3] Experimental studies with inhaled CO in quantities comparative to those found in cigarette smoke, have demonstrated a reduction in exercise tolerance in patients with angina pectoris, intermittent claudication and chronic obstructive pulmonary disease (COPD).[4-6]

Smoking is associated with elevated blood viscosity due to long term exposure to CO and, by an unclear mechanism,[7] an increased fibrinogen level. The elevated viscosity of blood is believed to contribute to platelet activation which promotes atherogenesis.[1,3] Cigarette smoke may promote arrhythmogenesis.[8] Smokers, on average, have a higher risk lipid profile than nonsmokers, this profile appears to reverse, in part, a couple of weeks after smoking cessation.[7]

For a more detailed review, on the specific mechanisms by which cigarette smoke contributes to acute vascular events and promotes atherosclerosis, we refer interested readers to Benowitz and Steven.[3]

### 1.2 Nicotine

Nicotine appears to be responsible for the haemodynamic effects associated with smoking and for coronary vasoconstriction. It has sympathomimetic effects that lead to increased HR and blood pressure and cause coronary vasoconstriction.[9]

Nicotine is liberated from the acid cigarette smoke as a gas, inhaled to the lungs, transferred via the alveoli to the blood, and is measurable in the CNS less than 8 seconds after inhalation.

All the nicotine replacement therapy (NRT) products that are used as an aid for smoking cessation are alkaline and therefore absorbed through the skin or mucous membranes. This route is much slower than by inhalation. Six hours after a transdermal patch of nicotine 21mg is applied, the blood concentration is approximately 10 to 17 µg/L in contrast with approximately 15 to 25 µg/L within minutes after a cigarette.[10]

It is likely that nicotine from cigarettes is more toxic than nicotine delivered from via NRT products such as patches. The rapid absorption from cigarette smoke results in a transient high blood concentration with a greater biological effect, compared with the equivalent dose of nicotine delivered from gums or patches.[11]

Compared with cigarette smoking, NRT produces lower plasma nicotine concentrations, i.e. one-third to one-half of the concentration attained over several hours, and does not produce high peak concentrations. The slower absorption of nicotine from these products does not produce the same cardiovascular stimulation as that delivered by cigarette smoke.[1]

### 1.3 Nicotine Replacement Therapy (NRT)

The rationale for nicotine substitution is as follows: when quitting smoking, the administration of nicotine via NRT decreases withdrawal symptoms in the first months, thus allowing the individual to cope with the behavioural and psychological aspects of smoking cessation. Lower nicotine concentrations are attained with NRT compared with smoking (i.e. the high peak plasma concentrations of nicotine reached during smoking are not achieved). Patients are weaned gradually from NRT products (usually over 2 to 6 weeks), in parallel with the decrease in withdrawal symptoms.

Without a certain element of instruction and support, NRT will not be efficacious. However, only 'minimal' behavioural therapy is required to increase cessation rates.[12] The degree of supportive adjunctive behavioural therapy parallels the factual success rates, while the relative success rate, i.e. the odds ratio between nicotine and placebo, remains more or less unchanged, around a factor 2.[12]

The average 12 month success rate reported in most studies of NRT is about 15 to 25%.[12] Results reported in a recent meta-analysis of 53 trials involving 17 703 individuals who received various forms of NRT (i.e. gum, patch, nasal spray and inhaler), indicated that NRT doubled long term (6 to 12 months) quit rates.[13] The odds ratio for success of NRT compared with placebo was 1.7 (95% confidence interval, 1.56 to 1.87). The odds ratio for the different nicotine replacement products were: 1.6 for gum; 2.1 for patch; 2.9 for nasal spray; and 3.1 for inhaler. No studies have directly compared the efficacy of different forms of NRT administration. However, data from three trials by Hjalmarson and colleagues in Sweden[14-17] using similar designs and adjunctive group therapy found remarkable consistency in 12 month success rates for nicotine gum (29%), nicotine nasal spray (27%) and nicotine inhaler (28%) with placebo rates of 16, 15 and 18%, respectively (table I). The high success rate in these studies reflects the magnitude of supportive behavioural programmes. Most NRT products are self-dosing systems to be used *ad libitum*, the exception is nicotine patches, which infuse nicotine at about 1 mg/h at a constant rate.

The classical relapse curve shows approximately 50% of smokers will have failed within the first 6 weeks after quit day on active drug and almost 75% on placebo. This suggests that healthcare providers should focus on an increase of NRT dose during the first weeks after quit day.

Minimal intervention with advice on how to quit smoking should also be included in the care of patients with cardiovascular disease (CVD). Prevention of cardiac disease by a broad

Table I. Percentage success rate from three placebo-controlled trials with nicotine chewing gum, spray and inhaler by Hjalmarson[17]

| Follow-up duration | Gum[a] | | Nasal spray[a] | | Inhaler[a] | |
|---|---|---|---|---|---|---|
| | nicotine (n = 106) | placebo (n = 100) | nicotine (n = 125) | placebo (n = 123) | nicotine (n = 123) | placebo (n = 124) |
| 6 wks | 77 | 52 | 53 | 27 | 46 | 33 |
| 3mo | 53 | 30 | 41 | 20 | 32 | 23 |
| 6mo | 37 | 20 | 35 | 15 | 35 | 19 |
| 12mo | 29 | 16 | 27 | 15 | 28 | 18 |
| a    All differences between nicotine and placebo were significant with $p < 0.05$. | | | | | | |

approach such as smoking cessation, education and legislation should also be an important goal for health authorities.

In sections 1.3.1 and 1.3.2, we review studies that have assessed the different forms of NRT in healthy individuals. Sections 2 and 3 focus on the few studies in which the effects of NRT were studied in patients with CVD.

### 1.3.1 Nicotine Transdermal Patch

The nicotine patch is a fixed nicotine delivery system which releases about 1mg of nicotine per hour for 16 hours (daytime patch) or for 24 hours (24-hour patch). NRT patches result in nicotine concentrations of approximately 50% of the concentrations achieved by smoking (21mg patch/24 hours and 15mg patch/16 hours). Patches are much easier to administer and to use compared with the gum, but it is not possible to self-titrate with patches.[18] The recommended treatment duration is 8 to 12 weeks.

In a multicentre smoking cessation trial from the US examining the effect of 0, 7, 14 and 21mg nicotine patches, a dose response effect was reported.[16] Two large placebo-controlled general practice trials comprising 600 and 1686 smokers have recently been published.[19,20] A 1-year success rate of 9.3% in the active patch group versus 5.0% in the placebo patch group was reported in first study[17] and a 3-month success rate of 14.4 versus 8.6%, respectively, was reported in the other study.[20] Among eight studies examining long term smoking cessation success, five showed a significant outcome in favour of the nicotine patch.[18]

Adverse effects are mainly mild local skin irritation, occurring in 5 to 10% of individuals. In only 1.5 to 2% of individuals, the patch had to be removed because of more persistent and severe local skin irritation.[18]

Because of its ease of use, the patch may be the first choice NRT. The patch has also been effective when combined with minimal supportive behavioural therapy. The findings from the two large trials in general practice[19,20] are also very encouraging. Transdermal NRT does increase success in smoking cessation with minimal adjunctive support.

### 1.3.2 Nicotine Chewing Gum, Nicotine Inhaler and Nicotine Nasal Spray

A basic advantage of these three products is the ability to self-titrate the dose, as opposed to the patch, which delivers a fixed dose. Thus, it is possible to administer a dose whenever wanted or needed during the day. Also, these products may replace some of the habit patterns associated with smoking (e.g. handling reinforcement) along with providing nicotine replacement. The principal disadvantage of these preparations is potential underdosing.

With use of nicotine gum throughout the day, blood concentrations of one-third (for 2mg gum) and two-thirds (for 4mg gum) of the nicotine obtained through smoking are achieved.[21-23] In most studies the gum has been used for at least 6 to 12 weeks and up to 1 year. Individualisation of treatment duration is recommended. Of the people who successfully quit smoking using nicotine gum, 10% will still use the gum after 12 months.

The nicotine inhaler contains small ampoules with nicotine and is similar in size and shape to a cigarette. The smoker can take a deep and intense or a more superficial 'draw' on the inhaler. Each ampoule contains about 10mg of nicotine in total and can release approximately 5mg nicotine. In clinical use, each ampoule releases approximately 1.5 to 2.0mg of nicotine and the number of nicotine ampoules used daily averages 5 to 6. Nicotine concentrations comparable to those found during use of the 2mg nicotine gum are attainable (i.e. relatively low concentrations). The mean nicotine substitution based on determinations after 1 to 2 weeks of therapy was 38 to 43% of nicotine concentrations achieved by smoking.[16,24]

The nicotine nasal spray (NNS) consists of a multidose, hand-driven pump spray containing a nicotine solution. Each puff contains nicotine 0.5mg, thus a 1mg dose is delivered if both nostrils are sprayed as recommended. The NNS is a rapid means of delivering nicotine into the human body with a pharmacokinetic profile closely approximating cigarettes. After a single dose of nicotine 1mg, peak concentrations of nicotine in plasma are reached within 5 to 10 minutes with average plasma trough concentrations of 16 $\mu$g/L after 4 to 6 hours.[25-27]

## 2. Efficacy of NRT in Patients with Coronary Heart Disease (CHD)

Interventions for smoking cessation after acute myocardial infarctions have achieved mixed results. Only a few studies have used NRT to achieve smoking cessation in patients with coronary heart disease (CHD). In a study by Taylor et al.[28] 5 patients with strong withdrawal urges were prescribed nicotine gum. Three of these patients stopped smoking. The study was not designed to determine the effect of NRT, but to determine the effect of a nurse-managed intervention for smoking cessation after a myocardial infarction. Only two randomised, placebo-controlled trials have been designed to determine the efficacy and safety of NRT in patients with CVD.

In 1996 Joseph et al.[29] published the results of a large randomised multicentre trial involving 584 smokers with CVD who received transdermal nicotine or placebo for 10 weeks (table II). Active treatment was given as a nicotine patch 21 mg/24h for 6 weeks, followed by tapering with a 14mg patch for 2 weeks and a 7mg patch for 2 weeks. After 14 weeks, the success rate was significantly higher (21%) in the nicotine group compared with the placebo group (9%). After 24 weeks, the abstinent rates were not significantly different. In this study, the long term quit rate was low compared with other trials in inpatients with acute cardiac disease. The authors of the study suggest that the high prevalence of coexisting psychiatric conditions (20%; 11% had depression and 9% had other psychiatric conditions) in the population of the study, and a history of numerous past failures to quit smoking, may explain this very low success rate. The fact that these patients were outpatients, and that this study was a multicentre study, might contribute to the low quit rates.

The Working Group for the Study of Transdermal Nicotine in Patients with Coronary Artery Disease[30] published the results of a 5-week randomised, placebo-controlled multicentre study. 156 patients with coronary artery disease were randomised to receive either placebo or transdermal nicotine 14mg per day. After 1 week, patients who had smoked more than 7 cigarettes since the beginning of the trial had their treatment dosage increased to 21 mg/day. The 5-week success rate was 36% in the NRT group and 22% in the placebo group (p < 0.05). There were large differences in the smoking cessation rates at different centres. The success rate in the NRT group varied between 18 and 67%, compared with 12 to 36% in the placebo

**Table II.** Clinical trials with nicotine patches in patients with cardiovascular disease

| Reference | No. of pts | Inclusion criteria | NRT | Duration | Smoking cessation success rate | Cardiac events/end-points |
|---|---|---|---|---|---|---|
| Joseph et al.[29] | 584 (male = 576), NRT = 294, Placebo = 290 | >15 cigarette/d over more than 5y; coronary artery stenosis (n = 63), angina pectoris (n = 211), arrhythmias (n = 86), cor pulmonale (n = 5), history of MI (n = 232), congestive heart failure (n = 74), peripheral vascular or cerebrovascular disease (n = 198) | 21 mg/24h patch for 6 wks, 14 mg/24h patch for 2 wks and 7 mg/24h patch for the last 2 wks | 10 wks | 14 weeks: 21% (NRT) vs 9% (placebo) [p = 0.001]; 24 weeks: 14% (NRT) vs 11% (placebo) [p = 0.67] | Primary end-points after 14 wks:[a] NRT group 5.4%; placebo group 7.9% (p = 0.23) Secondary end-points after 14 wks:[b] NRT group: 12% placebo group: 9.7% (p = 0.37) |
| Working Group for The Study of Transdermal Nicotine in Patients with Coronary Artery Disease[30] | 156 (male = 124), NRT = 62, Placebo = 62 | >20 cigarettes daily; history of MI (n = 115), stable angina (n = 83), bypass surgery (n = 53), angioplasty (n = 49), claudication (n = 32) | 14 mg/24h patch for 1 wk, then 21 mg/24h patch for 4 wks | 5 wks | After 5 wks: NRT group 36% Placebo group 22% (p < 0.05) | No significant differences in angina frequency, overall cardiac symptoms, arrhythmias, ischaemic ST segment depression |

a  Primary end-points: death, myocardial infarction, cardiac arrest, admission to hospital due to increased severity of angina, arrhythmia or congestive heart failure.

b  Secondary end-points: admission to hospital for other reasons and outpatient visits necessitated due to increased severity of heart disease.

NRT = nicotine replacement therapy; MI = myocardial infarction.

group. This study did not report follow-up after 5 weeks. This is important since only a small nonsignificant difference between nicotine and placebo treatment was observed in the study by Joseph et al.[29] after 24 weeks. Both studies found that nicotine patches increase short term success rate, i.e. 5 to 14 weeks. Almost all of the patients in these two studies were male, but no differences are mentioned in smoking cessation rates between males and females.

It should be noted that the efficacy (and safety) of nicotine chewing gum, inhaler and nasal spray has not been assessed in patients with CVD.

## 3. Safety of NRT in Patients with CHD

Whether nicotine increases the risk of CVD in humans is debatable. Smokers of cigarettes with high nicotine content do not experience more CHD than those who smoke cigarettes with low nicotine yields.[31] In a 12-year follow-up study of 136 000 Swedish construction workers, the relative risk of dying due to CVD was 2.1 among smokeless tobacco users, and 3.2 in smokers of 15 cigarettes/day or more, compared with nonusers.[32] However, in a study by Huhtasaari et al.,[33] it appeared that Swedish users of smokeless tobacco, who ingest similar amounts of nicotine to smokers, do not have a higher incidence of CHD than nonusers.

### 3.1 Clinical Trials

As mentioned in section 2, only two randomised, placebo-controlled trials have been published to determine the tolerability of NRT in patients with CVD. Both studies used nicotine patches. Patients who had recently had a myocardial infarction or whose cardiac status was significantly compromised were excluded from the study.

In the study by Joseph et al.,[29] adverse events (sleep disturbances, skin reaction, gastrointestinal distress) occurred in 12.2% of patients receiving NRT and in 9.3% of patients receiving placebo (p = 0.25). This study found no significant differences between the active and placebo group in occurrence of primary or secondary end-points (table II). The proportion of primary end-points was greater in the placebo group. Deaths were more common in the placebo group (p = 0.07).

In the other study,[30] patients underwent a 12-lead electrocardiogram (ECG) at a minimum of 3 points. At one centre, 24-hour ambulatory ECG monitors were worn by all patients over 3 weeks. The study indicated no increase in angina frequency, overall cardiac symptom status, nocturnal cardiovascular events or ECG changes (p < 0.05) associated with transdermal nicotine therapy, even in patients who continued to smoke intermittently.

The conclusion of both randomised placebo-controlled studies was that nicotine patches were well tolerated by patients with stable coronary disease.

### 3.2 Long Term Use of NRT and Incidence of Cardiovascular Events

Only one study, the Lung Health study[13,21] has investigated the long term use of nicotine medications. The aim of the study was not to examine the safety of NRT in patients with CVD, but to examine the effect of smoking cessation on lung function. 3923 patients with mild chronic pulmonary disease were followed for 5 years, and were offered nicotine 2mg chewing gum for variable time periods in a nonrandomised way. Many of these individuals used the gum heavily for several years. The rate of hospitalisation for cardiovascular conditions and cardiovascular deaths was not related to use or dosage of nicotine gum, or to concomitant use of nicotine gum and cigarettes. On the basis of these results, the investigators concluded that long term use of nicotine gum appears to be well tolerated.

### 3.3 Experimental Studies

A recent prospective study used exercise thallium-201 single photon emission computed tomography (SPECT) to assess sequential changes in myocardial ischaemia in patients before and during nicotine patch therapy.[34] The study group consisted of 36 patients, mean age 55 years, smoking more than 1 pack of cigarettes per day, with coronary artery disease on angiography and an abnormal SPECT. Patients were started on nicotine 14mg patches, and after approximately 1 week SPECT was repeated. They were then given nicotine 21mg patches, followed by a third exercise SPECT.

A significant reduction in the total perfusion defect size was observed during NRT, despite an increase in treadmill exercise duration and higher nicotine concentrations than when they were smoking. The patients reduced their smoking by 74%, and there was a significant correlation between the reduction in defect size and exhaled CO levels.

*In conclusion*, nicotine patches, compared with cigarette smoking, significantly reduce the extent of exercise-induced myocardial ischaemia. This study further suggests that CO, and possibly other components of cigarette smoke, rather than nicotine, may actually be more critical for the development of myocardial ischaemia. Although the overall results of this study are compelling, the lack of a placebo control group limits conclusions regarding the interplay between nicotine and CO, and their individual effect on myocardial ischaemia.

### 3.4 Case Reports

Case reports are by their nature retrospective, and lack controls. They will be mentioned, but they are of little value.

There is still concern by physicians regarding nicotine treatment in patients with coronary disease. Much of the concern stems from five case reports.[35] Full details of these cases have not been published, but they were carefully reviewed by a US Food and Drug Administration advisory committee and judged not to be causally related to nicotine.[36] As cardiovascular events are common in cigarette smokers, and the increased risk for such events persist beyond the time when they quit, it is impossible to ascertain from retrospective reports whether acute cardiovascular events reflect the risk of cigarette smoking, NRT, alone or in combination, or possible underlying disease. The available prospective epidemiological data suggest that smoking cessation is accompanied by a halving of the risk of CHD after 1 year, but that an additional 15 years are required for the risk to decline to the level of someone who has never smoked.[37]

Thirteen cases of cardiovascular events in people using NRT have been published,[38-47] including 3 cases of atrial fibrillation, 5 cases of myocardial infarction, 4 cases of cerebral ischaemia and 1 case of aortic dissection. In at least 4 of the cases there was concomitant cigarette smoking while using NRT. Most of the patients experienced the serious adverse event after many days' use of nicotine therapy, but in 6 cases there was a close temporal relationship. In 2 of the cases the patients used 2mg nicotine gum, 1 of them used 30 pieces of gum daily. The rest of the patients with reported serious adverse events used patches, 2 of them high-dose 44mg patches.

Brenner et al.[48] assumed that the myocardial infarction mortality is 1.3 times higher for smokers compared with the general US population. Taking into account the under reporting of adverse drug reactions and the actual use of NRT, there was no evidence of an increased risk of myocardial infarction due to transdermal nicotine according to adverse drug reaction reports.

## 4. Special Problems in Patients with CHD

The aim of this section is to give a detailed overview of the use of NRT in patients with specific cardiac problems. This section refers to the two clinical trials[29,30] (table II) mentioned in section 3, and reports on subsets of those patient cohorts.

### 4.1 NRT in Patients with Ischaemic Heart Disease

#### 4.1.1 Myocardial Infarction
Many prospective epidemiological studies have shown substantially lower rates of re-infarction, sudden cardiac death and total mortality in patients who quit smoking after acute myocardial infarction.[49-53] In one study,[54] patients who stopped smoking after myocardial infarction had half the mortality of those who continued to smoke.

In the two randomised studies[29,30] of nicotine patches in patients with CHD, 177 patients with myocardial infarction started nicotine patch treatment at least 2 weeks, in one study, and 3 months, in the other, after the cardiac event. No significant difference in cardiac morbidity or mortality was found in the nicotine-treated group compared with the placebo group.

#### 4.1.2 Angina Pectoris/Unstable Angina
Cigarette smoking is associated with increased risk of vasospastic angina and a poor response to medications in patients with vasospastic angina.[55,56] In one of the studies of NRT in patients with CHD,[30] 105 patients with angina were randomised to receive transdermal nicotine patches, although patients with unstable angina within the 2 weeks before randomisation were not included. Enrolled patients reported an average of 2 episodes per week, and took an

average of 2 sublingual nitroglycerin (glyceryl trinitrate) tablets per week. The majority of the individuals reported having angina only with hard work. The severity of angina increased and required hospital admission in 7% of the nicotine group and 10% of the placebo group. In the study by Joseph et al.,[29] 39 patients with stable angina were randomised to transdermal nicotine therapy. The mean number of attacks declined in both the treatment and the placebo group, as did episodes of ischaemic ST segment depression.

## 4.2 Arrhythmic Events and NRT

### 4.2.1 Arrhythmia and Malignant Arrhythmia

Cigarette smoking is a well known risk factor for sudden cardiac death, but the pathogenesis of this is incompletely understood. Cigarette smoking increases plasma levels of catecholamines that are potentially arrhythmogenic, especially in persons with ischaemic heart disease.

In the CAST study, which involved almost 1026 smoking high risk patients with frequent ventricular ectopic activity and left ventricular dysfunction after acute myocardial infarction,[57] smoking cessation was accompanied by a marked reduction in arrhythmic death and overall mortality.

In one of the randomised nicotine patch studies,[30] 43 patients with arrhythmia were included; however, patients who had been hospitalised for cardiac arrhythmia within the last 2 weeks were excluded.

In the other randomised study,[29] arrhythmia was not an inclusion criteria, but patients with serious ventricular arrhythmias and second-degree or higher atrioventricular block were excluded. As mentioned in section 3.1, ECG monitoring was performed. No patients receiving transdermal nicotine had a new onset of atrial or ventricular ectopy, or showed a statistically significant change from baseline at any week. The only change was for mean HR, which fell from 77 to 73 beats per minute at the end of week 1 in the placebo group.

In a study by Stein et al.,[58] 54 current smokers had 24-hour ECG recordings. They then attended smoking cessation classes and used transdermal nicotine patches while abstaining from smoking. After 4 to 6 weeks of abstinence the 24-hour ECG was repeated. Use of transdermal nicotine patches resulted in an improvement in indices of HR and HR variability compared with smoking ECG recordings.

HR variability based on normal R to R intervals were recorded. Indices of HR variability reflect cardiac autonomic tone, and decreased HR variability has been associated with high mortality after myocardial infarction[59] and sudden death in patients with ischaemic heart disease.[60]

## 5. Smoking Cessation in Patients with Cardiovascular Disease (CVD)

It is our personal experience that direct confrontation with a personal risk factor is a strong motivating factor. All patients with CVD are confronted with personal risk factors such as their blood pressure and serum cholesterol level. If the patient with CVD is a smoker, measurement of CO in expiratory air should be included as a vital sign whenever the healthcare system is in contact with him or her to attract attention to the need for smoking cessation. A CO value below 10 ppm is found in most nonsmokers, although the CO values in abstainers after 1 year most often range between 1 and 4 ppm.

Because it is important to get patients with CVD to quit smoking, long term NRT should be considered as a substitute for smoking in patients less motivated to quit smoking.

In patients not willing to quit smoking and/or pay for NRT an alternative might be to switch to smokeless tobacco. Although this might seem controversial, this is a practical approach which might be of benefit for hard core/recalcitrant smokers with CVD. For individual smokers not motivated to quit smoking, replacing cigarettes with smokeless tobacco will decrease their risk of cardiovascular diseases as well as the risk of COPD and lung cancer. These potential benefits greatly exceed the risk of oral cancers from long term use of smokeless tobacco (snuff). The alternative is often that the patient continues to smoke cigarettes. Thus, smokeless tobacco would likely be a less harmful option for this group of smokers.

In rehabilitation programmes smoking cessation must be included also, because smoking cessation is a factor affecting survival in patients with CVD.

The staff treating patients with CVD should be trained formally in smoking cessation, and attend yearly 'booster' courses.

## 5.1 Recommendations for Doses and Duration of NRT in Patients with CVD

Because of the few studies of NRT in patients with CVD the following recommendations are not based on hard evidence. We have drawn parallels from findings in healthy individuals, but more controlled studies with NRT in patients with CVD are needed to support these guidelines. However, it is well documented that smoking cessation *per se* improves the prognosis in patients with CVD.

Nicotine patches are the preferred form of NRT for these patients. The standard patch should be used, i.e. the 15mg daytime patch or the 21mg 24-hour patch, for 8 to 12 weeks for patients smoking >9 cigarettes daily. NRT has not been properly tested in individuals smoking fewer cigarettes (table III).

Although nicotine patches were first administered 2 weeks after acute myocardial infarction in the two trials,[29,30] we cannot see any contraindications to initiating patch treatment 2 to 3 days after acute myocardial infarction, as the alternative most often is cigarette smoking. Most patients with myocardial infarction will not smoke for the first few days after the acute event; thus, nicotine tolerance might be lost. When the patch treatment starts it might thus be advisable to use a smaller nicotine patch dose for the first 1 to 2 days, i.e. 10 mg/16 hour patch and 14 mg/24 hours patch and then use a standard dose after 1 to 2 days if no adverse events are observed. In patients admitted to hospital with unstable angina or malignant/severe arrhythmia the same precautions should be taken. Most outpatients continue to smoke until the planned quit day and start with a nicotine patch on quit day.

In patients with intolerable local adverse effects from the patch an alternative might be nicotine chewing gum (2mg; 5 to 15 pieces daily), for up to 12 to 24 weeks or the nicotine inhaler (4 to 10 ampoules daily) for the same period. Both the 2mg gum and the inhaler produce slow and low nicotine concentrations and might be well tolerated alternatives to patch treatment. However, no controlled trials with preparations other than the patch have been reported.

Nicotine nasal spray preparations should not be used until tested in controlled trials in patients with CVD due to the higher acute peak nicotine concentrations. Combined use of the patch and gum/inhaler is not advisable; however, a switch from patch to either gum or inhaler seems acceptable.

Use of NRT concomitantly with cigarette smoking appeared to be well tolerated in the Lung Health Study and might be used in a transition phase from reduced smoking to complete abstinence.[61] A new concept involves reducing the number of daily cigarettes to less than

**Table III.** Recommendations for the use of nicotine replacement therapy (NRT) to assist in smoking cessation in individuals with cardiovascular disease (CVD)

1. Smoking cessation should be included in all programmes of rehabilitation
2. Use carbon monoxide measurement for monitoring abstinence
3. Consider nicotine substitution:

| | Our proposal: | Documentation: |
|---|---|---|
| No. of cigarettes smoked daily | At least 10 | At least 15 |
| MI | Can be used 2-3 days after the acute MI | Has been used 2 wks after acute MI |
| Angina pectoris | Can be used in all patients | Has not been used in patients hospitalised with unstable angina in the last 2 wks |
| Arrythmia | Can be used in all patients | Has not been used in patients with serious ventricular arrhythmia, second-degree or higher AV-block or hospitalised for arrhythmia within the last 2 wks |
| NRT | **Nicotine patches** | |
| | Dosage: 15 mg/16h or 21 mg/24h | 21 mg/24h used in patients with CVD |
| | Duration: 8 (-12) weeks | Effects shown over 5-10 wks |
| | Patients who have not smoked for the last few days: 10 mg/16h or 14 mg/24h for 2 days then as mentioned above | |
| | **Nicotine chewing gum** | |
| | Dose: 2mg, 5-15 pieces daily | Not tested in patients with CVD |
| | Duration: 12-24 wks | |
| | **Nicotine Inhaler** | Not tested in patients with CVD |
| | Dose: 10mg, 4-10 ampoules/day | |
| | Duration: 12-24 wks | |

4. Alternatively consider smokeless tobacco in the recalcitrant smoker
5. Arrange follow-up (telephone, mail, clinic visit)

**AV** = atrioventricular; **MI** = myocardial infarction.

50% of baseline. Whether or not reduced smoking with the help of NRT products is a possible alternative in the recalcitrant smoker who is unable to stop smoking will be evaluated by several ongoing studies.

Follow-up visits should be arranged approximately 1 week after the quit day and then eventually after 2 to 3 weeks, 4 to 6 weeks and 10 to 12 weeks. Nurse-conducted telephone follow-up as well as letters have been used with success in patients with myocardial infarction, with reported long term quit rates double the normal.[62]

It is also mandatory that patients are asked about smoking by their doctor at every clinic visit, and undergo measurement of expired CO.

## 6. Conclusion

Smoking cessation has a positive effect on prognosis in patients with CHD and should have a high priority. In this group of patients, NRT in the form of nicotine patches seems to be well tolerated and to increase short term quit rates compared with placebo, although long term quit rates are not different from placebo. However, only 2 placebo-controlled trials of NRT have been conducted in this patient population and further studies of all types of NRT should be performed.

Further research should be directed towards NRT in smokers with acute myocardial infarction during initial hospitalisation and testing of 'minimal' versus 'extensive' behavioural support in conjunction with NRT with special focus on long term quit rates. A great educational and motivational task is to ensure that all healthcare professionals deliver state-of-the-art assistance regarding smoking cessation to all their patients with CHD who smoke. The healthcare system should make institutional changes to ensure the systematic identification and intervention of all tobacco users with CHD at every contact.

## References

1. Benowitz NL. Smoking-induced coronary vasoconstriction: implications for therapeutic use of nicotine. J Am Coll Cardiol 1993; 22 (3): 648-9
2. Department of Health and Human Services. The health consequences of smoking: cardiovascular disease: a report of the surgeon General. Washington, DC: Government Printing Office, 1983; (DHHS Publication no (PH5) 50204)
3. Benowitz NL, Steven G. Cardiovascular Toxicity of nicotine: implications for nicotine replacement therapy. J Am Coll Cardiol 1997; 29 (7): 1422-31
4. Allred EN, Bleecker ER, Chaitman BR, et al. Short-term effects of carbon monoxide exposure on the exercise performance of subjects with coronary artery disease. N Engl J Med 1989; 321 (21): 1426-32
5. Aronow WS, Cassidy J, Vangrow JS, et al. Effects of cigarette smoking and breathing carbon monoxide on cardiovascular hemodynamics in angial patients. Circulation 1974; 50: 340-7
6. Calverly PMA, Leggett RJE, Flenley DC. Carbon monoxide and exercise tolerance in chronic bronchitis and emphysema. BMJ 1981; 283: 878-80
7. Smith JR, Landaw SA. Smokers polycythemia. N Engl J Med 1978; 298: 6-10
8. Stubbe I, Eskilsson J, Nilsson-Ehle P. High-density lipoprotein concentrations increase after stopping smoking. BMJ 1982; 284: 1511-3
9. Kajser L, Berglund B. Effects of nicotine on coronary blood-flow in man. Clin Physiol 1985; 5: 541-52
10. Palmer KJ, Brickley MM, Faulds D. Transdermal nicotine. A review of its pharmacodynamic and pharmacokinetic properties and therapeutic efficacy as an aid to smoking cessation. Drugs 1992; 44 (3): 498-529
11. Porchet HC, Benowitz NL, Scheiner LB, et al. Apparent tolerance to the acute effect of nicotine results in part from distribution kinetics. J Clin Invest 1987; 80: 1466-71
12. Fiore MC, Bailey WC, Cohen SJ, et al. Smoking cessation. Clinical practice guideline No 18, AHCPR 96-0692. Rockville: U.S. Department of Health and Human Services, Public Health Service, Agency for Health Care Policy and Research, 1996
13. Silagy C, Mant D, Fowler G, et al. Meta-analysis on efficacy of nicotine replacement therapies in smoking cessation. Lancet 1994; 343: 139-42
14. Hjalmarson A. Effect of nicotine chewing gum in smoking cessation: a randomized, placebo-controlled, double-blind study. JAMA 1984; 252: 2835-8
15. Hjalmarson A, Franzon M, Westin A, et al. Effect of nicotine nasal spray on smoking cessation. Arch Intern Med 1994; 154: 2567-72
16. Hjalmarson A, Nilsson F, Sjostrom L, et al. The nicotine inhaler in smoking cessation. Arch Int Med 1997; 157 (5): 1721-8
17. Hjalmarson A. Smoking cessation. Evaluation of supportive strategies with special reference to nicotine replacement therapy [thesis]. Goteborg: Goteborg University, 1996
18. Fagerström KO, Säwe U, Tønnesen P. Therapeutic use of nicotine patches: efficacy and safety. J Smok Relat Dis 1992; 3: 247-61
19. Russell MAH, Stableton JA, Feyerabend C, et al. Targeting heavy smokers in general practice: randomised controlled trial of transdermal nicotine patches. BMJ 1993; 306: 1308-12
20. Imperial Cancer Research Fund General Practice Research Group. Effectiveness of a nicotine patch in helping people to stop smoking: results of a randomised trial in general practice. BMJ 1993; 306: 1304-8
21. McNabb ME, Ebert RV, McCusker K. Plasma nicotine levels produced by chewing nicotine gum. JAMA 1982; 248: 865-8
22. McNabb ME. Chewing nicotine gum for 3 months: what happens to plasma nicotine levels?. Can Med Assoc J 1984; 131: 589-92
23. Tønnesen P, Fryd V, Hansen M, et al. Two and four mg nicotine chewing gum and group counseling in smoking cessation: an open, randomized, controlled trial with a 22 month follow-up. Addict Behav 1988; 13: 17-27
24. Tønnesen P, Nørregaard J, Mikkelsen K, et al. A double-blind trial of a nicotine inhaler for smoking cessation. JAMA 1993; 269: 1268-71
25. Tønnesen P. Smoking cessation programs. In: Hansen HH, editor. Lung cancer. Boston (MA): Kluwer, 1994: 75-89
26. Sutherland G, Stapleton JA, Russell MAH, et al. Randomised controlled trial of a nasal nicotine spray in smoking cessation. Lancet 1992; 340: 324-9
27. Blondal T, Franzon M, Westin A, et al. Controlled trial of nicotine nasal spray with long term follow-up [abstract]. ARRD 1993; 147: A806
28. Taylor CB, Houston-Miller N, Killen JD, et al. Smoking cessation after acute myocardial infarction: effects of a nurse managed intervention. Ann Intern Med 1990; 113 (2): 118-23
29. Joseph AM, Norman SM, Ferry LH, et al. The safety of transdermal nicotine as an aid to smoking cessation in patients with cardiac disease. N Engl J Med 1996; 335: 1792-8
30. Working Group for the Study of Transdermal Nicotine in Patients with Coronary Artery Disease. Nicotine replacement therapy for patients with coronary artery disease. Arch Intern Med 1994; 154: 989-95
31. Hughes JR. Risk-benefit of nicotine replacement in smoking cessation. Drug Saf 1993; 8 (1): 49-56

32. Bolinder GM, Ahlborg BO, Lindell JH, et al. Use of smokeless tobacco: blood pressure elevation and other health hazards found in a large-scale population survey. J Intern Med 1992; 232 (4): 327-34

33. Huhtasaari F, Asplund K, Lundberg V, et al. Tobacco and myocardial infarction: is snuff less dangerous than cigarettes? BMJ 1992; 305 (6864): 1252-6

34. Mahmarian JJ, Moye LA, Nasser GA, et al. Nicotine patch therapy in smoking cessation reduces the extent of exercise-induced myocardial ischemia. J Am Coll Cardiol 1997; 30: 125-30

35. Hwang SL. Heart attacks reported in patch users still smoking. Wall Street Journal 1992 Jun 14

36. U.S. Food and Drug Administration. Transcript of the 23rd Meeting of the U.S. Food and Drug Administration. U.S. Food and Drug Administration, 1992

37. The Health Benefits of Smoking Cessation. Rockville, MD: US Dept of Health and Human Services, Public Health Service, Centers for Disease Control, Center for Chronic Disease Prevention and Health Promotion, Office on S Smoking and Health; 1990. US Dept of Health and Human Services Publication (CDC) 90-8416

38. Rigotti NA, Eagle KA. Atrial fibrillation while chewing nicotine gum [letter]. JAMA 1986; 225: 1018

39. Stewart PM, Caterall JR. Chronic nicotine ingestion and atrial fibrillation. Br Heart J 1985; 54; 222-3

40. Ottervanger JP, Jeroen MF, de Vries AG. Acute myocardial infarction while using nicotine patch. Chest 1995; 107: 1765-6

41. Dacosta A, Guy JM, Tardy B, et al. Myocardial infarction and nicotine patch: a contributing or causative factor? Eur Heart J 1993; 14: 1709-11

42. Warner JG Jr, Little WC. Myocardial infarction in a patient who smoked while wearing a nicotine patch. Ann Intern Med 1994; 120; 695-6

43. Jorenby DE, Smith SS, Fiore MC, et al. Varying nicotine patch dose and type of smoking counseling. JAMA 1995; 274: 1347-52

44. Pierce JR. Stroke following application of a nicotine patch [letter]. DICP 1994; 28; 402

45. Jackson M. Cerebral arterial narrowing with nicotine patch. Lancet 1993; 342; 236-7

46. Canadian adverse drugs reaction newsletter. Drugs directorate. Can Med Assoc J 1996 Jan 1; 154 (1): 61

47. Ropchan GV, Sanfilippo AJ, Ford SE. Aortic dissection and use of the nicotine patch: a case involving a temporal relationship. Can J Cardiol 1997; 13 (5): 525-8

48. Brenner DE, Pethica D, Mickhail HMI, et al. Surveillance of the cardiovascular safety of transdermal nicotine as smoking cessation aid [abstract]. Pharmacoepidemiol Drug Saf 1994; 3 Suppl. 1: 93

49. Aberg A, Bregstrand R, Johansson S, et al. Cessation of smoking after myocardial infarction. Effects on mortality after 10 years. Br Heart J 1983; 49: 416-22

50. Baile WF, Bigelow GE, Gottlieb SH, et al. Rapid resumption of cigarette smoking following myocardial infarction: inverse relation to MI severity. Addict Behav 1982; 7: 373-80

51. Daly LE, Mulcahy R, Graham IM, et al. Long term effect on mortality of stopping smoking after unstable angina and myocardial infarction. Br Med J (Clin Res) 1983; 287: 324-6

52. U.S. Dept of Health and Human Services. The health consequences of smoking: cardiovascular disease. A report of the Surgeon General. Rockville, MD: Dept of Health and Human Services, 1983; DHSS (PHS) no. 84-50204

53. Wilhelmsson C, Vedin JA, Elmfeldt D, et al. Smoking and myocardial infarction. Lancet 1975; I: 415-9

54. Mulcahy R. Influence of cigarette smoking on morbidity and mortality after myocardial infarction. Br Heart J 1983; 49: 410-5

55. Raymond R, Lynch J, Underwood D, et al. Myocardial infarction and normal coronary arteriography: a 10-year clinical and risk analysis of 74 patients. J Am Coll Cardiol 1988; 11: 471-7

56. Caralis DG, Ubeydullah D, Kern MJ, et al. Smoking is a risk factor for coronary spasm in young women. Circulation 1992; 85: 905-9

57. Peters RW, Brooks M, Todd L. Smoking cessation and arrhythmic death: the CAST experience. J Am Coll Cardiol 1995; 26: 1287-92

58. Stein PK, Rottman JN, Kleiger RE. Effect of 21mg transdermal nicotine patches and smoking cessation on heart rate variability. Am J Cardiol 1996; 77 (9): 701-5

59. Kleiger RE, Miller JP, Moss AJ, et al. Decreased heart rate variability and its association with increased mortality after acute myocardial infarction. Am J Cardiol 1987; 59: 256-62

60. Singer DH, Martin GL, Magid N, et al. Low heart rate variability and sudden cardiac death. J Electrocardiol 1988; 21: s46-55

61. Murray RP, Bailey WC, Daniels K, et al. Safety of nicotine polacrilex gum used by 3,094 participants in the Lung Health Study. Chest 1996; 109: 438-45

62. Barr Taylor C, Huston-Miller N, Killen JD, et al. Smoking cessation after acute myocardial infarction: effects of a nurse-managed intervention. Ann Intern Med 1990; 113 (2): 118-23

Correspondence: Dr P. *Tønnesen*, Medical Department of Pulmonary Medicine, Gentofte University Hospital, Niels Andersensvej, 2900 Hellerup, Denmark.
E-mail: pt0563@hotmail.com

# The Benefits of Stopping Smoking and the Role of Nicotine Replacement Therapy in Older Patients

*Steven G. Gourlay*[1] and *Neal L. Benowitz*[2]

1 National Heart Foundation of Australia Ralph Reader Overseas Research Fellow, University of California, San Francisco, California, USA
2 Division of Clinical Pharmacology and Experimental Therapeutics, University of California, San Francisco, California, USA

The aim of this review is to critically discuss the benefits of stopping smoking, and the efficacy, safety and clinical aspects of nicotine replacement therapies in older patients. Unless otherwise defined, 'older patients' are those aged 65 years or more. Most of the epidemiology and treatment literature report investigations were conducted in younger patient populations. In some cases, these data are used to extrapolate to older patients.

Rather than review data on the pharmacology of nicotine in younger people, readers are referred to several reviews of the subject.[1-4] This discussion focuses on aspects of pharmacology most pertinent to older smokers.

## 1. Epidemiology of Smoking

A substantial proportion of the older population continue to smoke despite the association of smoking with poorer health ratings.[5] Smoking prevalence data at different ages from the 1991 US National Health Survey[6] are shown in figure 1. The rates of smoking in the older population are lower compared with younger age groups due to stopping smoking and premature death from smoking-related diseases.

On average, older smokers smoke the same number or fewer cigarettes per day than younger smokers. The proportion of heavy smokers is lowest in older smokers.[5,7,8] These data may indicate a trend toward lower levels of nicotine dependence in older smokers, although data on nicotine dependence other than self-reported tobacco consumption from randomly selected population samples are not available.

Data from a non-randomly selected

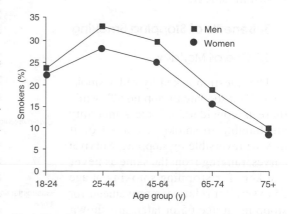

**Fig. 1.** Prevalence of smoking in the US among men and women as measured by the National Health Interview Survey, 1991 (n = 43 732).[6]

**Table I.** Usual time between waking and the first cigarette of the day among volunteers (smokers of ≥15 cigarettes/day) participating in a study of transdermal nicotine by age group[9]

| Age (y) | Time to first cigarette [number (%) of men] | | | Time to first cigarette [number (%) of women] | | |
|---|---|---|---|---|---|---|
| | >30 min | 6-30 min | ≤5 min | >30 min | 6-30 min | ≤5 min |
| 18-39 | 92 (28.5) | 125 (38.7) | 106 (32.8) | 113 (28.6) | 161 (40.9) | 120 (30.5) |
| 40-59 | 68 (22.9) | 124 (41.8) | 105 (35.3) | 70 (17.9) | 159 (40.8) | 161 (41.3) |
| 60-69[a] | 8 (21.0) | 15 (39.5) | 15 (39.5) | 7 (17.9) | 21 (53.9) | 11 (28.2) |

a   There were no statistically significant differences in the proportion of men or women aged 60 to 69y who smoked within 5 min of waking and younger smokers.

population sample suggest that older, moderate to heavy smokers requesting assistance to stop smoking have similar levels of nicotine dependence to younger smokers. In a large cohort of community volunteers for a study of transdermal nicotine,[9] the mean (± SD) Modified Fagerström Tolerance Scores[10] of men aged 60 to 69 years (n = 38) compared with men aged 18 to 39 years (n = 323) were 7.1 ± 1.7 and 6.8 ± 1.4 points, respectively (difference not significant). For women the scores were 6.6 ± 1.8 (n = 39) and 6.4 ± 1.8 (n = 394) (difference not significant) [Gourlay, unpublished data]. These individuals smoked ≥15 cigarettes per day, were highly motivated to stop smoking and had similar demographic characteristics to general practice-based smoking studies. The proportions of smokers who smoked soon after waking were also similar across the age groups (table I).

## 2. Risks of Smoking

Doll et al.[11] followed a cohort of 35 000 male doctors for 40 years and comprehensively documented many associations of smoking and disease, all of which became more common in older populations. In the 65 to 84 years age group, a 2-fold excess of mortality attributable to smoking was observed. Put another way, at age 70 years, the probability of surviving to 85 years is 41% in non-smokers compared with 21% in smokers. A list of smoking-related illnesses is shown in table II.

## 3. Benefits of Stopping Smoking

### 3.1 Overall Mortality

The question asked by older smokers is 'Is it too late to stop now?'; while there is considerable excess mortality attributable to smoking, not all of it may be reversible by stopping. Survival curves, ranging from the same as never smokers for stopping smoking at age 35 to smaller relative improvements for stopping at age 65 or later, are shown in figure 2. At first glance this figure paints a pessimistic picture for older

**Table II.** Smoking-related illnesses[11-15]

| Type | Disease |
|---|---|
| Cancer | Oesophageal |
| | Stomach |
| | Pancreatic |
| | Rectal |
| | Anal |
| | Pharyngeal |
| | Laryngeal |
| | Lung |
| | Bladder |
| | Cervical |
| | Vulval |
| | Penile |
| | Acute leukaemias |
| Cardiovascular | Ischemic heart disease |
| | Congestive cardiac failure |
| | Aortic aneurysm |
| | Cor pulmonale |
| | Stroke |
| | Peripheral vascular disease |
| Gastrointestinal | Peptic ulcer |
| Lung | Chronic obstructive pulmonary disease |
| | Pneumonia |
| Skeletal | Osteoporosis |

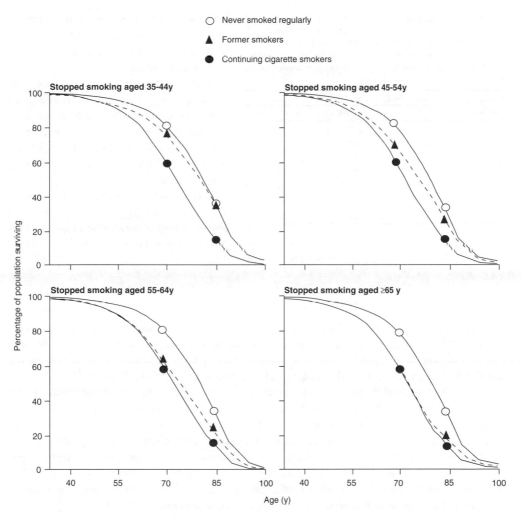

Fig. 2. Effects on survival after ages 45, 55, 65 and 75 years of stopping smoking in previous decade (reproduced from Doll et al.,[11] with permission).

smokers. However, in absolute terms, the number of premature deaths prevented by stopping smoking is similar across middle and older ages because of the higher burden of smoking-related disease in older smokers (table III).

Despite the likelihood of improved survival after stopping smoking, for the patient who enjoys smoking, it is reasonable to consider whether their quality of life, or quality-of-life–adjusted survival, can really be improved. Let us assume that stopping smoking at age 70 years improves survival by 20%, based on the survival curves shown in figure 2. If a smoker considered a life without smoking to be worth 80% or less of a life with continued smoking, there would be no mortality benefit to stopping, although improvements in morbidity are not considered by this argument (table IV). For stopping smoking at younger ages, when the

**Table III.** Average reduction in deaths 12.5y after stopping smoking among former moderate to heavy smokers [≥20 (women) or ≥21 (men) cigarettes/day] compared with continuing smokers (modified from tabulations from the American Cancer Society[16] to reflect 12.5y follow-up at all ages of stopping smoking, assuming death rates were constant during follow-up)

| Age at stopping smoking (y) | No. fewer deaths per 1000 | | |
|---|---|---|---|
| | men | women | combined |
| 40-44 | 53 | 30 | 83 |
| 45-49 | 83 | 61 | 144 |
| 50-54 | 92 | 76 | 168 |
| 55-59 | 99 | 91 | 190 |
| 60-64 | 38 | 45 | 83 |
| 65-69 | 23 | 152 | 175 |
| 70-74 | 60 | 106 | 166 |

survival curves of former smokers more closely approximate those of never smokers, quality-of-life adjustment will be less influential.

From the epidemiologist's point of view, quality of life is improved after stopping smoking because of reduced age-specific risks of cardiovascular disease and decreased lifetime incidence of cancer.[17] On the basis of this evidence it is hard to imagine many clinical situations where quality-of-life issues should stop health practitioners from recommending a serious attempt at stopping smoking. However, quality of life is not a trivial issue to patients and should be considered as part of any evaluation and follow-up for smoking.

## 3.2 Cardiovascular Disease

The relative risk of cardiovascular mortality among older smokers compared with non-smokers is in the order of 1.6, i.e. there is an excess mortality of 60% attributable to smoking.[18-20] Results from the Framingham study[21] suggest a lower relative risk but may have been biased by the classification of ex-smokers with smoking-related diseases as non-smokers.[11,22]

Excess cardiovascular disease risk imparted by smoking is reversed substantially by stopping smoking, even after the age of 65 years.[19,20,23] Because smoking is known to accelerate atherosclerosis this seems somewhat improbable. However, many of the effects of smoking on the cardiovascular system are mediated by short term mechanisms, including activation of the adrenergic nervous system,[3] coronary vasoconstriction,[24-27] adverse changes to the lipoprotein profile,[28,29] oxidative modification of lipoproteins,[30,31] endothelial damage,[32,33] activation of leucocytes[34] and other prothrombotic effects.[33,35-37] Improvement in many of these factors has been shown within days of stopping smoking completely.[34,38,39]

**Table IV.** Estimates of quality of life when stopping smoking at age 70y

| Probability of surviving 15y[a] (%) | | Quality-of-life factor (QLF) | Change in quality-of-life–adjusted survival[b] (%) |
|---|---|---|---|
| smoking | not smoking | | |
| 25 | 30 | 1.2 | +44 |
| 25 | 30 | 1.0 | +20 |
| 25 | 30 | 0.8 | –4 |
| 25 | 30 | 0.5 | –40 |

a    Probability of survival based on data from Doll et al.[11]

b    Change in quality-of-life–adjusted survival =

$$\left( \frac{\text{probability of survival not smoking}}{\text{probability of survival smoking}} \times QLF \times 100 \right) - 100$$

### 3.2.1 Atherosclerosis

Long term exposure to tobacco contributes to the development of atherosclerosis at many sites. Smoking is more strongly associated with aortic and peripheral arterial atherosclerosis[40-43] than with disease of the coronary and cranial circulations. The reason for the predilection of smoking-related damage for certain arterial sites is unclear.

Carotid atherosclerosis is less in former smokers than in current smokers.[44] It is probable that reduced atherosclerosis seen in such cross-sectional studies is due to reduced lifetime exposure to tobacco smoke rather than a significant reduction in the size of plaques after stopping smoking.[45-46] Studied prospectively, former smokers appear to be subject to a persistently elevated risk of aortic atherosclerosis, albeit reduced compared with that of current smokers.[42]

It is reasonable to conclude from the evidence discussed above that stopping smoking is accompanied by a rapid, partial reversal of cardiovascular risk, due primarily to reversal of the prothrombotic effects of smoking. In the long term, progression of underlying atherosclerotic disease is likely to be slowed.

### 3.2.2 Coronary Heart Disease

A well-designed prospective cohort study of asymptomatic men aged 65 to 74 years[18] found the rate of coronary heart disease for former smokers to be intermediate between those of current and never smokers during 12 years of follow up. The relative risks of smoking for coronary disease were similar for older smokers [1.6, 95% confidence interval (CI) 1.0 to 2.6] and middle-aged groups (1.8, 95% CI 1.3 to 2.6). However, the event rates were approximately twice as high in older smokers due to a higher underlying prevalence of coronary disease. This means that the number of cases attributable to smoking was greatest in older smokers.

Even stopping smoking at the time of myocardial infarction, cardiac surgery or coronary angioplasty can improve prognosis (based on patient populations with mean ages of 49 to 57 years). The rate of reinfarction after thrombolytic therapy for myocardial infarction is reported to be considerably lower if patients stop smoking at diagnosis (5.1% *vs* 20% for continued smokers).[47] In that study, neither the severity of angiographically determined disease nor any other factor apart from smoking was predictive of reinfarction. Restenosis after coronary angioplasty appears to be somewhat less frequent if patients stop smoking (38% *vs* 55%).[48] Improved survival has been demonstrated if patients stop smoking after undergoing coronary artery bypass surgery (80% *vs* 69% for continued smokers).[49]

An 18% reduction in coronary disease mortality has been demonstrated in a randomised trial of advice to stop smoking among men aged 40 to 59 years. These data confirm that stopping smoking itself, and not just coincident modification of other risk factors, reduces coronary risk.[50]

### 3.2.3 Stroke

Few studies of stroke restricted to older patients are available. The following discussion is mainly based on studies of all adult age groups[44,46,51-53] or of middle-aged patients.[54,55] As the incidence of stroke and suspected carotid artery disease increases with age, the age distributions of the cases reported by these studies are skewed towards older age.

Cigarette smoking is an important risk factor for ischaemic or haemorrhagic stroke and transient ischaemic attack.[16,52,54] Smoking is a stronger[44,53,55] or equally strong[46] predictor of carotid atherosclerosis than the other principal risk factors, hypertension and male gender. For thromboembolic and lacunar stroke combined, the relative risk of smoking has been reported to be as high as 5.7.[52] A meta-analysis of cohort and case-control studies reported the relative risk of smoking for combined stroke in smokers aged 55 to 74 years to be 1.8.[56]

Studies considering the benefits of stopping smoking on stroke report complete or partial reversal of risk within 5 to 10 years of stopping.[16] In one case-control study, the risk of stroke declined slowly after stopping smoking but some risk was still present at 10 years.[52] Other studies have reported more rapid acquisition of benefit. Greater prior cigarette consumption is associated with higher stroke risk among former smokers.[57] Reduced cerebral perfusion associated with smoking is substantially, but not completely, reversed within 12 months of stopping smoking.[51] Presumably, this indicates that the risk of stroke from smoking includes a substantial, reversible component and a longer-lasting, structural component.

### 3.2.4 Peripheral Vascular Disease

Improved resting ankle pressures and exercise tolerance have been demonstrated in patients (mean age 60 years) with established peripheral vascular disease who stop smoking over a 10-month period.[58] Reduced mortality, incidence of rest pain and amputations among patients with symptomatic disease after stopping smoking have also been demonstrated.[59-61] The patency rates of femoropopliteal grafts[62] and arteriovenous fistulae[63] are reduced among patients who continue to smoke compared with those who stop.

## 3.3 Pulmonary Disease

### 3.3.1 Lung Cancer

The increase in relative risk for lung cancer caused by smoking is higher than for any other smoking-related condition,[11] although in numerical terms, cardiovascular deaths from smoking are more common because of the higher incidence of cardiovascular events in the population.[64]

There are definite benefits of stopping smoking on lung cancer risk in older patients.[16,65] The absolute amount of risk reduction due to stopping may be greater for older smokers than for younger smokers because the incidence of lung cancer is higher in the older population.[66] A 50% risk reduction has been shown 10 to 15 years after stopping smoking at age 60 to 64 years.[67]

For patients with primary small-cell lung cancers, stopping smoking may reduce the incidence of second primary tumours in those achieving long term remission.[68]

### 3.3.2 Chronic Obstructive Pulmonary Disease

Average measures of forced expiratory volume in one second ($FEV_1$) are reduced in older, asymptomatic current or ex-smokers, indicative of a degree of obstructive pulmonary disease.[69-71] A cross-sectional study of $FEV_1$ in smokers aged 65 years or more showed that former smokers had no reduction in $FEV_1$ if they stopped smoking by age 40 years, slight reduction if they stopped by age 60 years, and moderate reduction (but still less than current smokers) if they stopped after age 60 years.[70] Older male ex-smokers appear to have the same rate of decline of lung function as never smokers, whereas that of smokers declines at a faster rate.[71]

These data suggest the main benefit of stopping smoking on lung function is to prevent further progression of lung damage, and to return the rate of decline in lung function with age toward normal. In addition, ex-smokers can expect improvement in airways symptoms such as nasal obstruction, cough, wheeze and dyspnoea.[16,50,71]

### 3.3.3 Surgical Complications

Smokers have higher rates of complications from major surgery than never smokers or former smokers. Patients undergoing coronary bypass surgery (mean age 64 years) are less likely to suffer pulmonary complications if they stop smoking for two months or more compared with continuing smokers (15% *vs* 57%).[72]

## 4. Role of Nicotine Replacement Therapy

Stopping smoking is not easy at any age. In patients aged 65 years and older, relatively high spontaneous smoking cessation rates of 9% per annum have been reported.[73] Assuming at least two-thirds of older smokers make a serious attempt to stop smoking each year,[74] this means that 87% of these smokers 'fail'. One of the reasons for failure may be nicotine withdrawal symptoms, which are strongest in the first 3 days after quitting and decline at a variable rate over subsequent weeks.[75] Craving for tobacco, irritability, other mood disturbances and problems sleeping are common complaints.[76] In addition, factors unrelated to nicotine dependence, such as lack of motivation, established behavioural patterns and social influences, may also reduce smokers' chances of successfully stopping smoking.

Nicotine withdrawal symptoms can be managed by non-pharmacological means, as evidenced by the majority of smokers who successfully stop smoking without formal assistance from health professionals, groups or pharmacotherapy. In most cases, smokers should be encouraged to cease smoking without incurring the additional expense and risk of pharmacotherapy. Brief, supportive counselling from a health professional may significantly improve smoking cessation rates (table V).[77]

Nicotine replacement therapy should be considered when older smokers fail to stop smoking by simpler means. Nicotine replacement assists smokers to stop smoking by reducing withdrawal symptoms and by diminishing the positive reinforcing effects of 'slip-up' cigarettes.[78-79]

If nicotine replacement therapy is used for light or occasional smokers (<10 cigarettes per day), or smokers who have abstained from nicotine for several days, it should be used cautiously. These smokers may not be as tolerant to the effects of nicotine as are more frequent smokers, so that nicotine replacement therapy may cause symptoms of nicotine excess such as nausea, vomiting and lightheadedness.

The efficacy of non-nicotine pharmacotherapy for stopping smoking is unproven by adequate randomised clinical trials. While clonidine reduces some nicotine withdrawal symptoms, it commonly causes adverse effects, can cause hypotension, and interacts with antidepressant and vasoactive drugs.[80] Falls are a serious problem for the elderly. Drugs that cause hypotension, such as clonidine, increase the risk of falls. Thus, clonidine is particularly unsuitable for older patients. Recent investigation of mecamylamine, a nicotinic receptor antagonist, has shown promise when combined with transdermal nicotine, but remains to be proven as a safe and effective treatment in the long term.[81] Mecamylamine, too, can cause orthostatic hypotension.

**Table V.** Brief (<10 min) nonpharmacological health professional intervention for smoking cessation[77]

| |
|---|
| Record smoking status |
| Personalise health effects of smoking |
| Give firm advice to stop smoking immediately |
| Provide self-help booklet |
| Determine if smokers are ready for action |
| Set quit day if motivated |
| Identify social support for cessation |
| Organise follow-up or referral |

## 5. Epidemiology of Nicotine Replacement Therapy

Little information is available about the use of nicotine replacement therapies other than transdermal nicotine in the community.

A pharmacy-based study of 1070 outpatients aged 65 to 74 years reported on the use of transdermal nicotine.[82] Most smokers who used the patches were nicotine dependent. The average duration of use was 5 weeks, 80% of patients started at the highest available dose (21 to 22 mg/24h), and 60% of patients who refilled their prescriptions did not change down to a lower dose. Most patients with a past history of myocardial infarction or heart disease (73%) started with the highest dose. In agreement with surveys of younger smokers,[83] approximately half of the patients smoked while wearing the patches, and this behaviour was strongly associated with long term relapse.

## 6. Treatment Issues in Older Patients

### 6.1 Does the Pharmacology of Nicotine Change with Aging?

No pharmacokinetic data for nicotine or its metabolites have been published for older patients. In the absence of these data, it is reasonable to hypothesise that the characteristics of nicotine absorption and elimination kinetics are unlikely to be changed to a clinically important extent in older patients.

The main reason for this assumption is that there is a high degree of interindividual variability in plasma nicotine concentrations during smoking or nicotine replacement therapy regardless of age.[84] This source of variability is likely to outweigh any changes related to aging. Secondly, absorption of highly lipophilic drugs, like nicotine, from the skin does not decrease as the skin ages and loses lipid content.[85] Similarly, absorption of nicotine from the lung or the mucous membranes of the mouth or nose is unlikely to change.

It is possible that aging could decrease the volume of distribution of nicotine because it is primarily distributed in lean body mass, which decreases with age. If the volume of distribution of nicotine is decreased then plasma nicotine concentrations after absorption from rapid nicotine delivery systems, such as nicotine gum or nasal spray, could increase. Steady-state plasma concentrations from slow delivery systems, such as transdermal nicotine, would not be affected as these concentrations are only determined by dose and clearance.

In support of the idea that the pharmacokinetics of nicotine do not change substantially with age, analysis of unpublished data from a cohort of transdermal nicotine users[9] confirms that plasma concentrations of nicotine and cotinine are similar across the age range of 18 to 69 years when individuals use the same dose nicotine patch (table VI).

### 6.2 Efficacy of Nicotine Replacement Therapy

#### 6.2.1 Randomised Clinical Trials

In general, reviews of randomised controlled studies of nicotine chewing gum or transdermal nicotine in all age groups estimate the efficacy of active nicotine therapy to be two-fold that of placebo.[86-89] Those evaluated generally smoked 10 or more cigarettes per day and were well motivated to stop smoking at the time of enrolment.

Placebo-controlled studies of smokers of 10 or more cigarettes per day with low nicotine dependence levels (classified by the Fagerström Tolerance Score[90]) disagree on the presence of a therapeutic effect of nicotine replacement treatment. Two of these studies reported no therapeutic effect of nicotine gum[91,92] and one found no effect of nicotine nasal spray in low dependence smokers.[93] In contrast, a placebo-controlled study of 16-hour transdermal nicotine therapy reported a substantial therapeutic effect, with a greater benefit in low compared with high dependence smokers.[94]

**Table VI.** Steady-state plasma concentrations of nicotine ($C^{ss}_{nic}$) and cotinine ($C^{ss}_{cot}$) and estimated plasma clearance values[a] by age group among individuals abstinent from tobacco[b] while using transdermal nicotine therapy 21 mg/24h[9] (mean ± SD)

| Parameter | Age group (y) | | |
|---|---|---|---|
| | 18-39 (n = 94) | 40-59 (n = 98) | 60-69 (n = 11) |
| Time since last patch applied (h) | 5.6 ± 3.8 | 5.9 ± 3.7 | 4.5 ± 2.4 |
| $C^{ss}_{nic}$ (ng/ml) | 9.8 ± 5.0 | 9.0 ± 5.2 | 9.0 ± 5.4 |
| $D/C^{ss}_{nic}$ (ml/min)[c] | 2110 ± 1641 | 2229 ± 1394 | 2137 ± 1049 |
| $D/C^{ss}_{nic}$ per kg (ml/min/kg) | 30.1 ± 25.4 | 32.4 ± 23.5 | 32.3 ± 18.1 |
| $C^{ss}_{cot}$ (ng/ml) | 170 ± 85 | 161 ± 72 | 167 ± 78 |
| $D/C^{ss}_{cot}$ (ml/min)[d] | 81.3 ± 50.2 | 82.5 ± 50.5 | 76.4 ± 36.9 |
| $D/C^{ss}_{cot}$ per kg (ml/min/kg) | 1.1 ± 0.7 | 1.2 ± 0.8 | 1.2 ± 0.6 |

a   Assuming the same dosage of nicotine (D) was absorbed and that the fractional conversion of nicotine to cotinine was similar in individuals of all ages, steady-state plasma concentrations ($C^{ss}$) of nicotine and cotinine are inversely proportional to plasma clearances ($CL^{ss}$): $CL^{ss} = D/C^{ss}$.

b   Individuals reported using transdermal nicotine for 24 h/day for at least 3 days without smoking during that time. Expired air carbon monoxide was ≤8 ppm on the day of measurement.

c   Estimated by the formula $D/C^{ss}_{nic} = 14583.33/C_{nic}$, assuming each individual received an average dosage of nicotine 21 mg/24h (14583.33 ng/min). The estimates are approximate because of unmeasured interindividual variation in the dose of nicotine absorbed from the transdermal patches and single point sampling of plasma nicotine.

d   Estimated by the formula $D/C^{ss}_{cot} = 14583.33 \bullet 0.72/C_{cot}$, assuming each individual received an average dosage of nicotine 21 mg/24h and the fractional conversion of nicotine to cotinine was 0.72.[89] The estimates are approximate because of unmeasured interindividual variability in the dose of nicotine absorbed and in the fractional conversion of nicotine to cotinine, and single point sampling of plasma cotinine.

No large randomised trials have been exclusively conducted in populations of older smokers, who may differ from younger smokers in important ways. As older smokers have a higher spontaneous stop smoking rate than younger smokers,[73] the effectiveness of stop smoking interventions may vary from that in younger populations. However, there is no *a priori* reason to believe that the efficacy of nicotine replacement should be lessened in older age.

A substantial proportion of older smokers are concerned about the prospects of nicotine withdrawal when they stop smoking.[95] They can expect to benefit symptomatically from a reduction of withdrawal symptoms in addition to the other positive effects of nicotine replacement therapy.

### 6.2.2 Cohort Studies and Surveys

Some information is available about nicotine replacement in older smokers from cohort and cross-sectional studies. Smokers of ≥15 cigarettes per day who were aged 40 years or more were shown to be more successful with transdermal nicotine treatment than younger subjects (25% *vs* 17%, p = 0.004).[9] The self-reported 6-month success rate of 29% for older smokers using transdermal nicotine from a pharmacy-based survey is promising, although subject to some exaggeration due to lack of biochemical confirmation of not smoking.[87]

### 6.2.3 Multicomponent Stop Smoking Programmes

Stop smoking programmes with behaviour modification components, such as multiple group counselling, in addition to nicotine replacement therapy report higher absolute success rates than those with brief counselling, although the odds ratios between nicotine and placebo groups are similar.[82,94,96] It is likely that more smokers will successfully abstain when additional programme components are added.[97] However, most smokers avoid group sessions or prolonged individual counselling.[74] For the majority, nicotine replacement treatment will consist of the product, the accompanying kit and brief counselling from their doctor and/or pharmacist.

## 6.3 Risks of Nicotine Replacement in Older Patients

### 6.3.1 Cardiovascular Disease

Consideration of cardiovascular disease is important in older patients because it is common and smokers may first present for assistance to stop smoking at the onset of symptoms indicative of underlying cardiovascular pathology.

Some physicians argue that the use of any nicotine in the presence of coronary disease is inadvisable.[98] However, in practice, smokers with coronary disease, unable to stop smoking by other means, may appropriately choose to reduce the harm from smoking by using nicotine replacement therapy.[99] Transdermal nicotine 14 to 21 mg/24h was well-tolerated in a randomised clinical trial of 159 patients with stable ischaemic heart disease.[100] In that trial, subjects (mean age 56 years) commenced with 14 mg/24h and were allowed to increase to 21 mg/24h after one week if they had smoked more than 7 cigarettes.

Most patients who have experienced an acute myocardial infarction will have passed their worst days of nicotine withdrawal and will have lost nicotine tolerance prior to discharge from hospital. These patients should be advised to try nonpharmacological stop smoking strategies initially.

There is no epidemiological evidence that nicotine replacement therapy increases the already elevated cardiovascular risk of smokers. In the case of transdermal nicotine, anecdotal reports of fatal and non-fatal acute myocardial infarction and worsening unstable angina received a flurry of media attention.[101] Considering the large population of smokers at high risk of coronary disease already treated in Europe and the US, the number of reports is substantially lower than predicted by population estimates.[102]

The harm of smoking is probably immediately reduced when smokers with coronary disease switch to nicotine replacement therapy (when not smoking concurrently) because carbon monoxide and other vasoactive compounds present in cigarette smoke are absent and the hypercoagulable state associated with smoking is reversed.[99] Even if smoking occurs, nicotine exposure is usually reduced. Nevertheless, it is appropriate to advise patients who complain of new or worsening ischaemic heart disease symptoms during nicotine replacement therapy to cease immediately and especially to stop smoking if they are still doing so.

### 6.3.2 Osteoporosis

It is unclear whether nicotine is the factor responsible for the association of smoking with osteoporosis. A recent study in mice reported decreased femoral bone density after oral nicotine treatment.[103] Alternative hypotheses include the effects of smoking to reduce bodyweight, and its anti-oestrogen effects.[104] Even if nicotine does adversely affect bone density, use of nicotine replacement products to stop smoking is likely to reduce the harm to bone from smoking, as nicotine intake is usually reduced during the attempt, or eliminated altogether if successful.

### 6.3.3 Sleep Disturbances

Difficulty sleeping is not uncommon after stopping smoking due to nicotine withdrawal. This issue may be particularly important for older smokers. Waking hours nicotine replacement therapy does not appear to adversely affect sleep but has not been prospectively compared with 24 hour therapy.[84,105,106] Transdermal nicotine patches worn for 24 hours cause predominantly mild symptoms of vivid dreaming or difficulty sleeping in approximately 12% of patients.[107-108] Thus, waking hours therapy may be best for those patients anticipated to experience insomnia.

### 6.3.4 Cutaneous Tolerability of Transdermal Patches

As skin ages it becomes thinner and loses adipose content.[90] It is plausible that adhesive from the patches could tear or damage delicate areas of skin if strongly adherent. Few data are available on the cutaneous tolerability of transdermal nicotine at different ages. In a cohort study of transdermal nicotine, those aged 40 to 70 years were less likely to report cutaneous reactions to the patches than younger individuals.[109] This effect may have been due to under-reporting of adverse experiences by older individuals but does suggest that cutaneous tolerability does not worsen with age.

## 6.4 Risks vs Benefits of Nicotine Replacement Therapy

The potential benefits to older smokers from stopping smoking are considerable. To assess the risk-benefit equation for nicotine replacement therapy several assumptions are necessary. These are:

- 1 in 10 to 20 smokers who use nicotine replacement therapy are helped to stop smoking permanently;[94]
- 1 in 2 patients will smoke during treatment;
- the rate of life-threatening adverse effects of treatment is close to zero;
- reversal of the prothrombotic effects of smoking is rapid after stopping smoking; and
- morbidity from other adverse effects is generally minor and is fully reversible once treatment is stopped.

The most important assumption is that virtually no life threatening adverse effects are attributable to treatment, since even a modest rate could offset the gains expected from the increased rate of stopping smoking. For healthy, medically stable patients, the risks of nicotine replacement are slight and outweighed by the benefits of stopping smoking.

Smokers with unstable coronary heart disease are probably the only subgroup of smokers at risk of clinically important adverse effects from treatment. However, the risk of nicotine replacement is likely to be substantially less than that of smoking, for reasons discussed previously. Patients with unstable coronary heart disease who smoke concurrently with treatment are commonly believed to be at particular at risk of exacerbation of myocardial ischaemia but it is unclear whether this risk is any greater than that incurred by smoking alone. If nicotine replacement therapy is used, dosage should be initially conservative, patients should be aware of the potential risks of smoking, and progress should be monitored carefully.

## 6.5 Selection of Nicotine Replacement Therapy

### 6.5.1 Type

There is no evidence favouring the efficacy of one form of nicotine replacement therapy over another. Therefore, the choice of therapy should be based on considerations of compliance and tolerability.

Once-daily administration with a transdermal patch is the simplest method of nicotine replacement and for this reason it is the treatment of choice for older patients. It also has the advantage of predictable dosing without the high peak plasma nicotine concentrations which characterise smoking or rapid nicotine delivery from other nicotine products.

Nicotine chewing gum is more difficult to use, particularly for older patients, because it sticks to dentures and it requires frequent dosing to obtain adequate plasma concentrations of nicotine. Sufficient consultation time and good comprehension are required to grasp the correct, slow chewing technique necessary to achieve good nicotine absorption from the buccal mucosa. Despite these limitations, nicotine gum is an effective form of nicotine replacement therapy for patients able to use it properly.[94]

Nicotine nasal spray and nicotine inhalers are newer forms of nicotine replacement therapy. Both require frequent dosing throughout the day. The irritant nature of the products to the upper respiratory tract[110-111] and the fine motor coordination required for their use makes them less appealing for older smokers.

The combination of 15 mg/16h transdermal nicotine and 2mg nicotine chewing gum has been shown to improve withdrawal symptoms[112] and to have an effect on smoking cessation rates.[113] However, these effects may have been due to the total dose of nicotine delivered rather than to the combination of different nicotine delivery systems.

### 6.5.2 Dosage

Recommended dosages of transdermal nicotine treatment consist of 4 to 12 weeks of 15 mg/16h patches or 21 to 22 mg/24h patches, followed by a variable weaning period of lower dosages. Studies of empirical 44 mg/24h transdermal nicotine therapy for moderate to heavy smokers have demonstrated better suppression of withdrawal symptoms and urges to smoke than a 22 mg/24h dosage but without substantially improved smoking cessation rates.[114,115]

Dosage dependent effects on smoking cessation rates have been demonstrated for nicotine chewing gum in highly nicotine dependent smokers[116] and transdermal nicotine therapy in the dosage range of 7 to 21 mg/24h.[96] When transdermal nicotine dosages are adjusted by the percentage 'replacement' of baseline plasma cotinine concentrations, 100% replacement is associated with improved smoking cessation rates compared with 50% replacement.[117]

For nicotine chewing gum, a dosage of at least 6 pieces per day is required to achieve optimal efficacy.[118]

### 6.5.3 Waking vs 24-Hour Use

Both 24-hour and waking hours (removed before sleep) transdermal treatment regimens were effective in clinical trials. One clinical study directly compared 24-hour and waking hours therapy and found no therapeutic differences but the study had low statistical power to detect small effects.[119] Assuming there are no major differences in efficacy between the two types of therapy, tailoring dosage to the individual is the most rational approach. For example, 24-hour therapy may be preferred by patients who experience strong urges to smoke first thing in the morning while waking hours therapy may be preferred by patients for whom sleep disturbance is an important issue. All of the commercially available transdermal nicotine patches deliver nicotine at similar average rates, so that all types can be used for waking hours therapy.

## 6.6 Drug Interactions

Smoking accelerates the hepatic metabolism of several classes of drugs;[3] this effect is mediated by the effects of polycyclic hydrocarbons rather than by nicotine. This is probably a dose-dependent effect, so that light smokers are less likely to be affected.

Moderate to heavy smokers who stop or reduce smoking may experience clinically important increases in plasma concentrations of drugs such as theophylline[120] and caffeine[121] (table VII). Increased caffeine concentrations after stopping smoking may contribute to the tobacco withdrawal syndrome via symptoms such as anxiety and restlessness.[123] Nicotine gum has been shown to have no effect on theophylline clearance.[120]

## 6.7 Dealing with Smoking or Relapse During Nicotine Replacement Therapy

Smoking concurrently with nicotine replacement therapy is inadvisable but a clinical reality, occurring in about 50% of cases, including in the elderly.[9,87,88] Patient progress should be reviewed after the first few weeks and those who have smoked more than a few times concurrently with treatment should probably discontinue nicotine replacement therapy and restart from a new quit day. Smoking more than 1 or 2 cigarettes concurrently with transdermal nicotine therapy is strongly associated with long term relapse to smoking.[9,87,124,125] While using nicotine replacement therapy, it is relatively easy to reduce the intake of tobacco because of the nicotine supplied by the product. However, unless smoking stops completely, the behavioural reinforcement of smoking continues.

# 7. Cost of Nicotine Replacement Therapy

The daily cost of nicotine replacement therapy in most countries is similar to that of a pack of cigarettes. The problem for older smokers, who may be financially disadvantaged, is finding the money to purchase the therapy in advance, as it is unusual for pharmaceutical schemes to cover the cost. Some private health insurance companies and health maintenance organisations provide coverage, although it may be conditional on enrolment in a formal stop smoking course.

In the light of data that the benefits of stopping smoking are substantial in older smokers, it is imperative that useful treatments for stopping smoking are provided in an affordable way for this economically disadvantaged sector of the community. Government and private health plans for the elderly are encouraged to include nicotine replacement therapy and other treatments for stopping smoking.

# 8. Conclusions

The benefits of stopping smoking are considerable for older smokers. The pharmacology of nicotine and tobacco is probably unchanged in clinically important ways with advancing age.

**Table VII.** Drugs with clinically significant increases in plasma concentrations after stopping smoking, irrespective of nicotine replacement therapy

| Drug | Change in plasma concentration | Suggested action |
|---|---|---|
| Caffeine | Increased[121] | Reduce to <4-6 cups of coffee/cola or soda/tea per day |
| | | Monitor compliance at follow-up |
| Propranolol | Increased[122] | Check degree of β-blockade |
| | | Reduce dose if patient excessively bradycardic |
| Theophylline | Increased[120] | Reduce dose |
| | | Monitor plasma concentrations at day 3 after stopping smoking |

Nicotine replacement therapy is a logical and effective approach for treating motivated, older smokers unable to quit by simpler means. Absolute success rates can be augmented by the inclusion of other interventions, such as counselling and follow-up support. Transdermal nicotine is the nicotine replacement therapy of first choice in older patients because of once-daily dosing and good tolerability. There are no significant risks of treatment in the absence of unstable coronary heart disease.

## Acknowledgements

Dr Gourlay and Professor Benowitz have been paid consultants to, and have received research funding from, pharmaceutical companies that market nicotine replacement products.

Preparation of this manuscript was supported in part by US National Institute of Drug Abuse grant DA02277.

## References
1. US Department of Health and Human Services. The health consequences of smoking and nicotine addiction: a report of the Surgeon General, 1988. Public Health Service, Centers for Disease Control, Center for Chronic Disease Prevention and Health Promotion, Office on Smoking and Health, 1988: DHHS Publication No. (CDC) 88-8406
2. Houezec J, Benowitz NL. Basic and clinical psychopharmacology of nicotine. Clin Chest Med 1991; 12: 681-699
3. Benowitz NL. Pharmacologic aspects of smoking. N Engl J Med 1988; 319: 1318-30
4. Benowitz NL. Pharmacology of nicotine: addiction and therapeutics. Annu Rev Pharmacol Toxicol 1996; 36: 597-613
5. Maxwell CJ, Hirdes JP. The prevalence of smoking and implications for the quality of life among the community-based elderly. Am J Prev Med 1993; 9: 338-45
6. US Department of Health and Human Services. Cigarette smoking among adults: United States, 1991. MMWR Morbid Mortal Wkly Rep 1993; 42: 230-3
7. Risk Factor Prevalence Study Management Committee. Risk factor prevalence study: survey no. 3 1989. Canberra: National Heart Foundation of Australia and Australian Institute of Health, 1990
8. University of California, San Diego. Tobacco use in California, 1990-1991. Sacramento: California Department of Health Services, 1992
9. Gourlay SG, Forbes A, Marriner T, et al. A prospective study of factors predicting smoking cessation using transdermal nicotine therapy. BMJ 1994; 309: 842-6
10. Gourlay SG, McNeil JJ. Antismoking products. Med J Aust 1990; 153: 699-707
11. Doll R, Peto R, Wheatley K, et al. Mortality in relation to smoking: 40 years' observations on male British doctors. BMJ 1994; 309: 901-11
12. Mellstrom D, Rundgren A, Jagenburg R, et al. Tobacco smoking, ageing and health among the elderly: a longitudinal study of 70-year-old men and an age cohort comparison. Age Ageing 1982; 11: 45-58
13. Colsher PL, Wallace RB, Pomrehn PR, et al. Demographic and health characteristics of elderly smokers: results from established populations for epidemiologic studies of the elderly. Am J Prev Med 1990; 6: 61-70
14. Daling JR, Sherman KJ, Hislop G, et al. Cigarette smoking and the risk of anogenital cancer. Am J Epidemiol 1992; 135: 180-9
15. Brownson RC, Novotny TE, Perry MC. Cigarette smoking and adult leukemia. Arch Intern Med 1993; 153: 469-75
16. US Department of Health and Human Services. The health benefits of smoking cessation: a report of the Surgeon General, 1990. US Department of Health and Human Services, Public Health Service, Centers for Disease Control, Center for Chronic Disease Prevention and Health Promotion, Office on Smoking and Health, 1990: DHHS Publication No. (CDC) 90-8416
17. Rose G, Shipley M. Effects of coronary risk reduction on the pattern of mortality. Lancet 1990; 335: 275-7
18. Benfante R, Reed D, Frank J. Does cigarette smoking have an independent effect on coronary heart disease incidence in the elderly? Am J Public Health 1991; 81: 897-9
19. LaCroix AZ, Lang J, Scherr P, et al. Smoking and mortality among older men and women in three communities. N Engl J Med 1991; 324: 1619-25
20. Jajich CL, Ostfeld AM, Freeman DH. Smoking and coronary heart disease mortality in the elderly. JAMA 1984; 252: 2831-4
21. Harris T, Cook EF, Kannel WB, et al. Proportional hazards analysis of risk factors for coronary heart disease in individuals aged 65 or older. J Am Geriatr Soc 1988; 36: 1023-8
22. Omenn GS, Hermanson B, Kronmal RA. Smoking cessation in older patients with coronary artery disease [letter]. N Engl J Med 1989; 320: 1149
23. Hermanson B, Omenn GS, Kronmal RA, et al. Beneficial six-year outcome of smoking cessation in older men and women with coronary artery disease. N Engl J Med 1988; 319: 1365-9
24. Deanfield JE, Shea MJ, Wilson RA, et al. Direct effects of smoking on the heart: silent myocardial ischemic disturbances of coronary flow. Am J Cardiol 1986; 57: 1005-9
25. Sugiishi M, Takatsu F. Cigarette smoking is a major risk factor for coronary spasm. Circulation 1993; 87: 76-9
26. Winniford MD, Jansen DE, Reynolds GA, et al. Cigarette smoking-induced coronary vasoconstriction in atherosclerotic coronary artery disease and prevention by calcium antagonists and nitroglycerin. Am J Cardiol 1987; 59: 203-7

27. Moreyra AE, Lacy CR, Wilson AC, et al. Arterial blood nicotine concentration and coronary vasoconstrictive effect of low-nicotine cigarette smoking. Am Heart J 1992; 124: 392-7
28. Craig WY, Palomaki GE, Haddow JE. Cigarette smoking and serum lipid and lipoprotein concentrations: an analysis of published data. BMJ 1989; 298: 784-8
29. Freeman DJ, Griffin BA, Murray E, et al. Smoking and plasma lipoproteins in man: effects of low density lipoprotein cholesterol and high density lipoprotein subfraction distribution. Eur J Clin Pharm 1993; 23: 630-40
30. Scheffler E, Wiest E, Woehrle J, et al. Smoking influences the atherogenic potential of low-density lipoprotein. Clin Investig 1992; 70: 263-8
31. Morrow JD, Frei B, Longmire AW, et al. Increase in circulating products of lipid peroxidation ($F_2$ – isoprostanes) in smokers. N Engl J Med 1995; 332: 1198-203
32. Celermajer DS, Sorensen KE, Georgakopoulos D, et al. Cigarette smoking is associated with dose-related and potentially reversible impairment of endothelium-dependent dilation in healthy young adults. Circulation 1993; 88: 2149-55
33. Smith FB, Lowe GDO, Fowkes FGR, et al. Smoking, haemostatic factors and lipid peroxides in a population case control study of peripheral arterial disease. Atherosclerosis 1993; 102: 155-62
34. McGill HC. The cardiovascular pathology of smoking. Am Heart J 1988; 115: 250-7
35. Kario K, Matsuo T, Nakao K. Cigarette smoking increases the mean platelet volume in elderly patients with risk factors for atherosclerosis. Clin Lab Haematol 1992; 14: 281-7
36. Salbas K. Effect of acute smoking on red blood cell deformability in healthy young and elderly non-smokers, and effect of verapamil on age- and acute smoking-induced change in red blood cell deformability. Scand J Clin Lab Invest 1994; 54: 411-16
37. Kannel WB, D'Agostino RB, Belanger AJ. Fibrinogen, cigarette smoking, and the risk of cardiovascular disease: insights from the Framingham study. Am Heart J 1987; 113: 1006-10
38. Feher MD, Rampling MW, Brown J, et al. Acute changes in atherogenic and thrombogenic factors with cessation of smoking. J R Soc Med 1990; 83: 146-8
39. Rabkin SW. Effect of cigarette smoking cessation on risk factors for coronary atherosclerosis. Arteriosclerosis 1984; 53: 173-84
40. Cole CW, Hill GB, Farzad E, et al. Cigarette smoking and peripheral arterial occlusive disease. Surgery 1993; 114: 753-7
41. Fowkes FGR, Housley E, Riemersma RA, et al. Smoking, lipids, glucose intolerance, and blood pressure as risk factors for peripheral atherosclerosis compared with ischemic heart disease in the Edinburgh artery study. Am J Epidemiol 1993; 135: 331-40
42. Witteman JCM, Grobbee DE, Valkenburg HA, et al. Cigarette smoking and the development and progression of aortic atherosclerosis. Circulation 1993; 88: 2156-62
43. Pathobiological Determinants of Atherosclerosis in Youth Research Group. Relationship of atherosclerosis in young men to serum lipoprotein cholesterol concentrations and smoking. JAMA 1990; 264: 3018-24
44. Tell GS, Howard G, McKinney WM, et al. Cigarette smoking cessation and extracranial carotid atherosclerosis. JAMA 1989; 261: 1178-80
45. Cook DG, Shaper AG, Pocock SJ, et al. Giving up smoking and the risk of heart attacks. Lancet 1986; II: 1376-80
46. Dempsey RJ, Moore RW. Amount of smoking independently predicts carotid artery atherosclerosis severity. Stroke 1992; 23: 693-6
47. Rivers JT, White HD, Cross DB, et al. Reinfarction after thrombolytic therapy for acute myocardial infarction followed by conservative management: incidence and effect of smoking. J Am Coll Cardiol 1990; 16: 340-8
48. Galan KM, Deligonul U, Kern MJ, et al. Increased frequency of restenosis in patients continuing to smoke cigarettes after percutaneous transluminal coronary angioplasty. Am J Cardiol 1988; 61: 260-3
49. Cavender JB, Rogers WJ, Fisher LD, et al. Effects of smoking on survival and morbidity in patients randomised to medical or surgical therapy in the coronary artery surgery study (CASS): 10 year follow-up. J Am Coll Cardiol 1992; 20: 287-94
50. Rose G, Hamilton PJS, Colwell L, et al. A randomised controlled clinical trial of anti-smoking advice: 10-year results. J Epidemiol Community Health 1982; 36: 102-8
51. Rogers RL, Meyer JS, Judd BW, et al. Abstention from cigarette smoking improves cerebral perfusion among elderly chronic smokers. JAMA 1985; 253: 2970-4
52. Donnan GA, McNeil JJ, Adena MA, et al. Smoking as a risk factor for cerebral ischaemia. Lancet 1989; II: 643-7
53. Homer D, Ingall TJ, Baker Jr HL, et al. Serum lipoproteins are less powerful predictors of extracranial carotid artery atherosclerosis than are cigarette smoking and hypertension. Mayo Clin Proc 1991; 66: 259-67
54. Buhler FR, Vesanen K, Watters JT, et al. Impact of smoking on heart attacks, strokes, blood pressure control, drug dose, and quality of life aspects in the international prospective primary prevention study in hypertension. Am Heart J 1988; 115: 282-8
55. Whisnant JP, Homer D, Ingall TJ, et al. Duration of cigarette smoking is the strongest predictor of severe extracranial carotid artery atherosclerosis. Stroke 1990; 21: 707-14
56. Shinton R, Beevers G. Meta-analysis of relation between cigarette smoking and stroke. BMJ 1989; 298: 789-94
57. Rogot E, Murray JL. Smoking and causes of death among US veterans: 16 years of observation. Public Health Rep 1980; 95: 213-22
58. Quick CRG, Cotton LT. The measured effect of stopping smoking on intermittent claudication. Br J Surg 1982; 69: S24-6
59. Faulkner KW, House AK, Castleden WM. The effect of cessation of smoking on the accumulative survival rates of patients with symptomatic peripheral vascular disease. Med J Aust 1983; 1: 217-9

60. Jonason T, Bergstrom R. Cessation of smoking in patients with intermittent claudication. Acta Med Scand 1987; 221: 253-60
61. Lepäntalo M, Lassila R. Smoking and occlusive peripheral artery disease. Eur J Surg 1991; 157: 83-7
62. Myers KA, King RB, Scott DF, et al. The effect of smoking on the late patency of arterial reconstructions in the legs. Br J Surg 1978; 65: 267-71
63. Wetzig GA, Gough IR, Furnival CM. One hundred cases of arteriovenous fistula for haemodialysis access: the effect of cigarette smoking on patency. Aust NZ J Surg 1985; 55: 551-4
64. Peto R, Lopez AD, Boreham J, et al. Mortality from smoking in developed countries 1950-2000. Oxford: Oxford University Press, 1994
65. Lubin JH, Blot WJ. Lung cancer and smoking cessation: patterns of risk. J Natl Cancer Inst 1993; 85: 422-3
66. Sobue T, Yamaguchi N, Suzuki T, et al. Lung cancer incidence rate for male ex-smokers according to age at cessation of smoking. Jpn J Cancer Res 1993; 84: 601-7
67. Halpern MT, Gillespie BW, Warner KE. Patterns of absolute risk of lung cancer mortality in former smokers. J Natl Cancer Inst 1993; 85: 457-64
68. Richardson GE, Tucker MA, Venzon DJ, et al. Smoking cessation after successful treatment of small-cell lung cancer is associated with fewer smoking-related second primary cancers. Ann Intern Med 1993; 119: 383-90
69. Gregg I, Nunn AJ. Peak expiratory flow in symptomless elderly smokers and ex-smokers. BMJ 1989; 298: 1071-2
70. Higgins MW, Enright PL, Kronmal RA, et al. Smoking and lung function in elderly men and women. JAMA 1993; 269: 2741-8
71. Sherrill DL, Lebowitz MD, Knudson RJ, et al. Longitudinal methods for describing the relationship between pulmonary function, respiratory symptoms and smoking in elderly subjects: the Tuscon study. Eur Respir J 1993; 6: 342-8
72. Warner MA, Offord KP, Warner ME, et al. Role of preoperative cessation of smoking and other factors in postoperative pulmonary complications: a blinded prospective study of coronary artery bypass surgery. Mayo Clin Proc 1989; 64: 609-16
73. Salive ME, Cornoni-Huntley J, LaCroix AZ, et al. Predictors of smoking cessation and relapse in older adults. Am J Public Health 1992; 82: 1268-71
74. Fiore MC, Novotny TE, Pierce JP et al. Methods used to quit smoking in the United States. JAMA 1990; 263: 2760-5
75. Hatsukami D, Hughes JR, Pickens R. Characterisation of tobacco withdrawal: physiological and subjective effects. In: Grabowski J, Hall SM, editors. Pharmcological adjuncts in smoking cessation. Research monograph 53. US Department of Health and Human Services, National Institute on Drug Abuse, 1985: DHHS Publication No. (ADM) 85-1333
76. American Psychiatric Association. Diagnostic and statistical manual of psychiatric disorders. 4th ed. Washington DC: American Psychiatric Association, 1994
77. Mattick RP, Baillie A, Grenyer B, et al. An outline for approaches to smoking cessation: quality assurance project [NCADA Monograph No. 19]. Mattick RP, Baillie A, editors. Canberra: Australian Government Publishing Service, 1992: 15-50
78. Foulds J, Stapleton J, Feyerabend C, et al. Effect of transdermal nicotine patches on cigarette smoking: a double blind crossover study. Psychopharmacology 1992; 106: 421-7
79. Levin ED, Westman EC, Stein RM, et al. Nicotine skin patch treatment increases abstinence, decreases withdrawal symptoms, and attenuates rewarding effects of smoking. J Clin Psychopharmacol 1994; 14: 41-9
80. Fagerström KO. Measuring the degree of physical dependence to tobacco smoking with reference to individualisation of treatment. Addict Behav 1978; 3: 235-41
81. Niaura R, Goldstein MG, Abrams DB. Matching high- and low- dependence smokers to self-help treatment with or without nicotine replacement. Prev Med 1994; 23: 70-7
82. Blondal T. Controlled trial of nicotine polacrilex gum with supportive measures. Arch Intern Med 1989; 149: 1818-21
83. Hjalmarson A, Franzon M, Westin A, et al. Effect of nicotine nasal spray on smoking cessation. Arch Intern Med 1994; 154: 2567-72
84. Sachs DP, Säwe U, Leischow SJ. Effectiveness of a 16-hour transdermal nicotine patch in a medical practice setting, without intensive group therapy. Arch Intern Med 1993; 153: 1881-90
85. Gourlay SG, Benowitz NL. Is clonidine an effective smoking cessation therapy? Drugs 1995; 50: 197-207
86. Rose JE, Behm FM, Westman EC, et al. Mecamylamine combined with nicotine skin patch facilitates smoking cessation beyond nicotine patch treatment alone. Clin Pharmacol Ther 1994; 56: 86-9
87. Orleans CT, Resch N, Noll E, et al. Use of transdermal nicotine in a state-level prescription plan for the elderly: a first look at 'real world' patch users. JAMA 1994; 271: 601-7
88. Haxby D, Sinclair A, Eiff MP, et al. Characteristics and perceptions of nicotine patch users. J Fam Pract 1994; 38: 459-64
89. Benowitz NL, Jacob III P. Metabolism of nicotine to cotinine studied by a dual stable isotope method. Clin Pharmacol Ther 1994; 56: 483-93
90. Roskos KV, Maibach HI, Bircher AJ, et al. The effect of aging on percutaneous absorption in man. J Pharmacokinet Biopharm 1989; 17: 617-30
91. Fiore MC, Jorenby DE, Baker TB, et al. Tobacco dependence and the nicotine patch. JAMA 1992; 268: 2687-94
92. Gourlay SG. The pros and cons of transdermal nicotine. Med J Aust 1994; 160: 152-9
93. Fagerström K-O, Sawe U, Tønnesen P. Therapeutic use of nicotine patches: efficacy and safety. J Smoking-Related Dis 1992; 3: 247-61
94. Silagy C, Mant D, Fowler G, et al. Meta-analysis on efficacy of nicotine replacement therapies in smoking cessation. Lancet 1994; 343: 139-42
95. Orleans CT, Rimer BK, Cristinzio S, et al. A national survey of older smokers: treatment needs of a growing population. Health Psychol 1991; 10: 343-51

96. Transdermal nicotine study group. Transdermal nicotine for smoking cessation. JAMA 1991; 266: 3133-8
97. Kottke TE, Battista RN, DeFriese GH, et al. Attributes of successful smoking cessation interventions in medical practice. JAMA 1988; 259: 2882-9
98. Arnaot MR. Nicotine patches may not be safe. BMJ 1995; 310: 663-4
99. Benowitz NL. Nicotine patches. BMJ 1995; 310: 1409-10
100. Working group for the study of transdermal nicotine in patients with coronary disease. Arch Intern Med 1994; 154: 989-95
101. Hwang SL, Waldholt M. Heart attacks reported in patch users still smoking. Wall Street Journal: June 19, New York 1992
102. Brenner DE, Pethica D, Mickail HMI, et al. Surveillance of the cardiovascular safety of transdermal nicotine as smoking cessation aid [abstract]. Pharmacoepidemiol Drug Saf 1994 Aug; 3 Suppl. 1: 593
103. Broulik PD, Jarab J. The effect of chronic nicotine administration on bone mineral content in mice. Horm Metab Res 1993; 25: 219-21
104. Baron JA, Kiel DP. Cigarette smoking and osteoporosis. J Smoking-Related Dis 1994: 5 Suppl. 1: 69-74
105. Tønnesen P, Nørregaard J, Simonsen K, et al. A double-blind trial of a 16-hour transdermal nicotine patch in smoking cessation. N Engl J Med 1991; 325: 311-5
106. Russell MAH, Stapleton JA, Feyerabend C, et al. Targeting heavy smokers in general practice: randomised controlled trial of transdermal nicotine patches. BMJ 1993; 306: 1308-12
107. Imperial Cancer Research Fund General Practice Research Group. Effectiveness of a nicotine patch in helping people stop smoking: results of a randomised trial in general practice. BMJ 1993; 306: 1304-8
108. Gourlay SG, Forbes A, Marriner T, et al. A randomised clinical trial of a second course of transdermal nicotine therapy. BMJ 1995; 311: 363-6
109. Gourlay SG. Pharmacotherapies for smoking cessation [thesis]. Melbourne: Monash University, 1995
110. Sutherland G, Stapleton JA, Russell MAH, et al. Randomised controlled trial of nasal nicotine spray in smoking cessation. Lancet 1992; 340: 324-9
111. Tønnesen P, Nørregaard J, Mikkelsen K, et al. A double-blind trial of a nicotine inhaler for smoking cessation. JAMA 1993; 269: 1268-71
112. Fagerström KO, Schneider NG, Lunell E. Effectiveness of nicotine patch and nicotine gum as individual versus combined treatments for tobacco withdrawal symptoms. Psychopharmacology 1993; 111: 271-7
113. Kornitzer M, Boutsen M, Dramaix M, et al. Combined use of nicotine patch and gum in smoking cessation: a placebo-controlled clinical trial. Prev Med 1995; 24: 41-7
114. Dale LC, Hurt RD, Offord KP, et al. High dose nicotine patch therapy: percentage of replacement and smoking cessation. JAMA 1995; 274: 1353-8
115. Jorenby DE, Smith SS, Fiore MC, et al. Varying nicotine patch dose and type of smoking cessation counselling. JAMA 1995; 274: 1347-52
116. Tønnesen P, Fryd V, Hansen M, et al. Effect of nicotine chewing gum in combination with group counselling on the cessation of smoking. N Engl J Med 1988; 318: 15-8
117. Sach DP, Benowitz NL, Bostrum AG, et al. Percent serum replacement and success of nicotine patch therapy [abstract]. Am J Respir Crit Care Med 1995; 151: A688
118. Killen JD, Fortmann SP, Newman B, et al. Evaluation of a treatment approach combining nicotine gum with self-guided behavioral treatments for smoking relapse prevention. J Clin Consult Clin Psychol 1990; 58: 85-92
119. Daughton DM, Heatley SA, Prendergast JJ, et al. Effect of transdermal nicotine delivery as an adjunct to low-intervention smoking cessation therapy: a randomized placebo-controlled, double-blind study. Arch Intern Med 1991; 151: 749-52
120. Lee BL, Benowitz NL, Jacob III P. Cigarette abstinence, nicotine gum and theophylline disposition. Ann Intern Med 1987; 106: 553-5
121. Brown CR, Jacob III P, Wilson M, et al. Changes in rate and pattern of caffeine metabolism after cigarette abstinence. Clin Pharm Ther 1988; 43: 488-91
122. Deanfield J, Wright C, Krikler S, et al. Cigarette smoking and the treatment of angina with propranolol, atenolol and nifedipine. N Engl J Med 1984; 310: 951-4
123. Benowitz NL, Hall SM, Modin G. Persistent increase in caffeine concentrations in people who stop smoking. BMJ 1989; 298: 1075-6
124. Kenford SL, Fiore MC, Jorenby DE, et al. Predicting smoking cessation: who will quit with and without the nicotine patch. JAMA 1994; 271: 589-94
125. Stapleton JA, Russell MAH, Feyerabend C, et al. Dose effects and predictors of outcome in a randomized trial of transdermal nicotine patches in general practice. Addiction 1995; 90: 31-42

Correspondence: Dr *Steven Gourlay*, UCSF Box 0898, San Francisco, CA 94143-0898, USA.

# Abuse Potential of Nicotine Replacement Therapies

*Harriet de Wit*[1] and *James Zacny*[2]

1 Department of Psychiatry, The University of Chicago, Chicago, Illinois, USA
2 Departments of Psychiatry and Anesthesia and Critical Care,
 The University of Chicago, Chicago, Illinois, USA

## 1. Rationale for Nicotine Replacement Therapies

Nicotine replacement therapies (NRTs) are popular, well tolerated and effective aids to the cessation of cigarette smoking and other forms of tobacco use.

NRT is based on the belief that nicotine is the ingredient in tobacco that maintains dependence on cigarette smoking.[1,2] NRTs provide nicotine-dependent individuals with nicotine in a form that is less harmful to the body than inhaled smoke.[3] The high toxicity of cigarette smoke is attributed to constituents of the smoke, such as tar and carbon monoxide, which are linked to serious diseases such as cancer and emphysema. Thus, NRTs are designed to satisfy the pharmacological basis of the addiction while minimising some of the most serious adverse health consequences of smoking.

## 2. Characteristics that Determine Abuse and Dependence Liability

Well tolerated and effective pharmacotherapies for drug abuse or dependence must themselves have low potential for abuse and dependence. Potential for abuse is of particular concern for pharmacotherapies that are designed to mimic or replace the abused or dependence-producing drug [e.g. methadone for the treatment of diamorphine (heroin) dependence]. By definition, any drug that shares pharmacological characteristics with an abused drug is itself considered to have some liability for abuse and dependence.

According to guidelines of the US Food and Drug Administration (FDA), abuse liability is determined by two main factors: (i) the likelihood of repeated use; and (ii) the incidence of adverse consequences.

The 'likelihood of repeated use' is thought to be mainly determined by the direct, pleasurable effects of the drug and by the degree to which it relieves withdrawal symptoms after repeated use. The likelihood of repeated use may also be limited by unpleasant effects (e.g. local irritation) that accompany drug administration.

The 'incidence of adverse consequences' refers to the harmful consequences of use; thus, drugs that produce greater adverse consequences, either short term (e.g. cognitive or psycho-motor impairment that is hazardous to the user or to others) or long term (e.g. medical complications of prolonged use), are considered to have a greater abuse liability than drugs with fewer adverse effects.

Because abuse liability is a relative concept, the abuse liability of a pharmacotherapy must be assessed in relation to a standard drug and its route of administration. In the case of nicotine, it seems reasonable to assess the dependence or abuse liability of NRTs in relation to the substance they are being used to treat, i.e. inhaled cigarette smoke. Therefore, in this review of the dependence and abuse liability of various NRTs, we will assess the likelihood of repeated use and the adverse consequences of each formulation of NRT in relation to cigarettes.

The relative abuse liabilities of the NRTs may be determined by several factors. One of the main dimensions on which the NRTs differ from one another and from inhaled smoke is in their pharmacokinetic profiles, in particular the rate at which effective concentrations are reached. Rapidity of onset is thought to be an important determinant of the abuse potential of drugs, including nicotine.[1,4-6] Inhaled smoke delivers nicotine to the brain extremely rapidly (i.e. within 10 to 20 seconds of inhalation[1]), whereas, for example, the transdermal nicotine system (nicotine patch) delivers nicotine much more slowly (i.e. 1 to 2 hours). Therefore, we shall pay particular attention to the pharmacokinetic properties of the various NRTs.

The NRTs can also be compared on several other aspects, such as:
- the degree to which they produce subjective reports of liking and euphoria
- the incidence of unpleasant side effects
- the total exposure to nicotine
- the difficulty in stopping after long term use.

Data are not available on all of these aspects for all the NRTs, but some of the most important differences will be discussed.

Nicotine is one of the few substances for which there is a DSM-IV[7] category of 'dependence' but no category of 'abuse'. Dependence refers to 'a cluster of cognitive, behavioural and physiological symptoms indicating that the individual continues use of the substance despite significant substance-related problems . . . a pattern of repeated self-administration that usually results in physical dependence, tolerance and compulsive drug-taking behaviour'. Abuse, on the other hand, refers to 'use leading to clinically significant impairment or distress', such as 'failure to fulfil major role obligations, . . . use in situations in which it is physically hazardous . . . and recurrent substance-related legal problems'.

Clearly, nicotine is unlike most other prototypic drugs of abuse because it is not thought to produce intoxication or significant cognitive or motor impairment, and because its use is legal. For these reasons there is no category of 'nicotine abuse'.

Although this assessment of dependence and abuse liability of NRTs focuses primarily on aspects of dependence, we will also refer to measures of abuse because information regarding the direct, mood-altering effects is directly relevant to continued use of the drugs.

## 3. Methods Used to Assess Dependence and Abuse Liability

### 3.1 Subjective Effects

One of the most widely accepted measures of abuse liability is the evaluation of the subjective effects of single doses of drugs.[8] Typically, in these studies individuals receive a drug and a placebo under double-blind conditions. They are instructed to rate the strength of any drug effects they experience, as well as the degree to which they like the effects of the drug and what class of drug they believe they received.

In addition, many investigators use other standardised questionnaires, such as the Profile of Mood States (POMS)[9] and the Addiction Research Center Inventory (ARCI)[10] to determine the qualitative characteristics of the psychoactive effects of drugs. Several of these questionnaires have subscales that are relevant to abuse liability. Ratings of drug liking and increased scores on the scales measuring drug-induced euphoria are considered to be indicators of potential for abuse.

There is some controversy about the degree to which nicotine produces pleasurable, 'euphorigenic' subjective effects in individuals who are dependent on it. On one hand, nicotine is not thought to produce the kind of clearly definable intoxication, or 'high', that is associated with other prototypic drugs of abuse, nor does it produce the psychomotor impairment that is usually associated with abused drugs.[11,12] Nevertheless, it has been shown that nicotine administered intravenously to cigarette smokers does produce increased ratings of drug liking,[13] and one recent study demonstrated increases in self-reported euphoria from smoked cigarettes.[14] Thus, subjective reports of liking and euphoria may be valid measures on which to assess the abuse potential of NRTs.

## 3.2 Adverse Effects

As mentioned in section 2, some pharmacotherapies may produce either short or long term adverse effects. The short term averse effects are likely to reduce the likelihood that the drug in a particular delivery system will be abused. The long term adverse effects of a proposed pharmacotherapy are relevant to the safety and overall acceptability of the therapy.

The adverse effects of prolonged exposure to nicotine from NRTs are not fully known. However, because NRTs involve the administration of the same active drug that is being abused, the long term effects resulting from prolonged exposure to nicotine through NRTs are unlikely to exceed the effects from exposure via cigarettes.

Nevertheless, there may be differences in the long term consequences of exposure with different NRTs and smoking because of differences in the pharmacokinetic profiles (e.g. cycling *vs* constant blood concentrations, adverse effects of routes of administration) of various formulations.

## 3.3 Choice Tests/Self-Administration

One way to assess the abuse potential of a drug is to measure the tendency of individuals to take the drug compared with a placebo under controlled laboratory conditions.

In choice tests or drug self-administration procedures, individuals are provided with the opportunity to consume drugs under conditions where doses of drugs and expectations about outcomes are controlled. Self-administration procedures are considered to be good indicators of the likelihood that a drug will be abused outside the laboratory.[15,16]

Although few such studies have been conducted with NRTs, they are nevertheless a valuable potential source of data regarding the likelihood of repeated use.

## 4. Nicotine Chewing Gum

### 4.1 Pharmacokinetics

Nicotine in gum is bound to an ion exchange resin and is released by chewing. The nicotine released from the gum is absorbed in the buccal cavity or is swallowed. Buccal absorption of nicotine from the polacrilex base is facilitated by an alkaline pH (i.e. 8.5).

The nicotine that is swallowed is broken down by first-pass metabolism in the liver, and 35 to 40% is available systemically.[17] Nicotine is mainly metabolised by the liver and to a lesser extent by the kidney and lungs. Principal metabolites of nicotine are cotinine and nicotine-1′-N-oxide. Both nicotine and its metabolites are excreted through the kidneys, with about 10 to 20% of the absorbed nicotine excreted unchanged in the urine. Metabolism of nicotine administered via gum approximates that of nicotine administered via tobacco smoke.[18]

Nicotine absorption via the buccal mucosa is slow, occurring gradually over 20 to 30 minutes. This is in contrast to inhaled smoke, where each puff produces a rapid 'spike' in plasma nicotine concentrations (see fig. 1). Exactly how much nicotine is available systemically depends largely on how the gum is chewed.

Benowitz et al.[17] examined blood concentrations of nicotine in 14 smokers who either chewed 12 pieces of 2 or 4mg nicotine gum or smoked *ad libitum* over a 12-hour period. Assays of the plasma concentrations of nicotine and its metabolites yielded two important findings: (i) extraction of nicotine from gum was incomplete and variable among individuals; and (ii) analysis of nicotine metabolite data revealed that some nicotine extracted from the gum was lost via incomplete absorption from the gastrointestinal tract. Further, the amount of nicotine that was systemically absorbed from the 2 and 4mg pieces of gum was approximately 1 and 2mg, respectively.

Although there was considerable variability among individuals, both doses produced an average plasma nicotine concentration that was less than that derived from smoking: about one-third of the plasma nicotine concentration from smoking for the 2mg gum and about two-thirds of that from smoking for the 4mg gum.

### 4.2 Direct Effects

#### 4.2.1 Subjective Effects

Several clinical studies have examined mood effects in abstinent smokers who were administered either placebo or nicotine chewing gum.[17,21-24] Compared with those individuals receiving nicotine gum, those who received placebo gum commonly reported higher ratings of irritability, anxiety, restlessness, difficulty concentrating and impatience. These symptoms are characteristic of nicotine withdrawal, and the nicotine gum appeared to relieve these aversive symptoms. Whether nicotine gum also

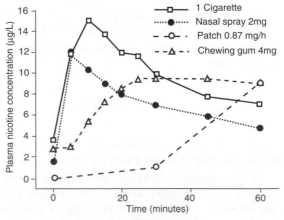

**Fig. 1.** Plasma concentrations of nicotine up to 60 minutes after administration of nicotine by various routes. Plasma concentrations are presented for 1 cigarette,[19] nicotine nasal spray,[20] a transdermal nicotine system[19] and nicotine chewing gum.[19]

produced hedonically positive affective states is difficult to determine from these studies.

Several studies have examined the subjective effects of nicotine gum in humans under controlled laboratory conditions. Although most studies have focused on smokers, one study[25] has examined the subjective effects of nicotine gum in nonsmokers in whom the effects of the nicotine product are unconfounded by the presence of physical dependence or nicotine withdrawal. In that study, individuals with little (n = 3) or no (n = 13) experience with tobacco chewed 0, 2 and 4mg of nicotine polacrilex across different sessions.

Measures of subjective effects included a short-form ARCI, two visual analogue scales that measured positive and negative effects of the nicotine gum, and a questionnaire that assessed the strength and liking of drug effects. The ARCI consisted of 40 true-false statements that comprised three scales:

- Morphine-Benzedrine Group (MBG) scale, a measure of euphoria
- Pentobarbital-Chlorpromazine-Alcohol Group (PCAG) scale, a measure of sedation
- Lysergic Acid (LSD) scale, a measure of dysphoria and psychotomimetic changes.[26,27]

Ratings of 'feel drug effect' and 'dose strength' were directly related to the dose of the nicotine gum. Individuals reported significant overall negative effects (as measured by a visual analogue scale) when chewing the active doses. Oddly enough, scores on the MBG scale of the ARCI were significantly increased by the 4mg dose. The authors speculated that this may have been due less to the euphoriant effects of the nicotine than to its stimulant effects.

The subjective effects of 4mg nicotine gum were examined in individuals who had been deprived of cigarettes for 10 hours.[28] Study participants were instructed to chew the gum at varying rates: 1 chew per 1, 2, 4 or 8 seconds. Measures included visual analogue scale ratings of positive and negative effects and the short-form ARCI. LSD scores increased significantly in individuals chewing at a rate of 1 chew per 1 second when compared with the scores obtained at the other 3 chewing rates, but no other differences were noted across conditions. This study was limited because no placebo gum was included to evaluate the drug effect.

In a study that did have a placebo gum group and similar subjective effect measures, drug liking scores did not differ between placebo and active drug doses.[29]

Finally, a more recent study[30] examined the mood of smokers under three conditions: after 2 days of tobacco smoking, 4 days of chewing 2mg gum and 4 days of complete nicotine abstinence. When individuals were switched from smoking to abstinence, nicotine withdrawal ratings reliably increased, as measured by scores on the POMS[9] and the Shiffman-Jarvik Tobacco Withdrawal Questionnaire.[31] However, when individuals were switched from smoking to nicotine gum chewing, no changes in mood were recorded.

The absence of an increase in dysphoria when smokers were switched from tobacco to nicotine gum suggests that replacement of nicotine during withdrawal prevents the mood changes and discomfort associated with withdrawal.[22-24,32,33] This mood stabilising effect may account, at least in part, for why a number of gum users have difficulty in weaning themselves from the gum.[34]

### 4.2.2 Reinforcing Effects (Self-Administration)

Hughes and his associates have conducted several studies to determine if nicotine gum serves as a reinforcer (i.e. to determine if active gum resulted in more self-administration than placebo gum).

In a laboratory study,[35] nonsmokers (i.e. those who had never smoked), ex-smokers and current smokers (tobacco-abstaining) sampled both nicotine (2mg) and placebo gum over two

4-hour periods (1 piece/hour) and were then given concurrent access to both gums. All three groups self-administered significantly less nicotine gum than placebo, suggesting that nicotine gum, in general, does not function as a reinforcer and is in fact aversive. Among the three groups, nonsmokers self-administered less nicotine gum than did current smokers, suggesting that the gum was more aversive in the former group. Consistent with this difference, the nonsmokers reported more dysphoric effects from nicotine gum than the other groups.

In a clinical study,[34] the reinforcing effects of placebo and three doses of nicotine gum were measured in 78 smokers who were trying to quit. Patients were randomly assigned to receive 0, 0.5, 2 and 4mg doses of nicotine gum. Use of the gum and withdrawal symptomatology were assessed at regular intervals over a 9-month period. Individuals in all four groups reported some withdrawal symptomatology during the first week of abstinence, but these symptoms dissipated soon thereafter.

However, the groups differed in their use of the gum well after the withdrawal symptoms had disappeared. Of the patients who successfully abstained from smoking after 6 months of treatment, those who were assigned to the 2 and 4mg doses were using more of the gum than those assigned to the 0 and 0.5mg doses. These differences suggest that the use of the gum was maintained by factors other than relief of withdrawal. Moreover, the relationship between frequency of use and dose of nicotine suggests that gum use was maintained by the positive reinforcing effects of nicotine.

Hughes et al.[35-37] have also demonstrated that the ability of nicotine gum to serve as a reinforcer can be modulated by instructional control. In one study, smoking cessation patients were either given correct instructions (e.g. 'you will receive nicotine gum' when they actually were given nicotine gum) or incorrect instructions (e.g. 'you will receive placebo gum' when they actually were given nicotine gum) or no information.[37] By the use of such a design, the independent impact of the pharmacological effects of nicotine and instructions could be assessed.

Individuals who were told they were receiving nicotine gum and did actually receive nicotine gum (2mg), self-administered more gum than individuals who were told they were receiving nicotine gum but in fact received placebo gum. In contrast, individuals who were told they were receiving placebo gum but actually received nicotine gum, self-administered less gum than individuals who were told they were receiving placebo gum and actually received placebo gum.

The authors related the differential use of nicotine gum to the notion that in one condition, individuals attributed stimulus effects of the nicotine gum to therapeutic efficacy (and thus used more gum), whereas in the other condition, individuals attributed the stimulus effects of the nicotine gum to adverse effects. Thus, depending on instructions and whether individuals believed they were receiving active drug, nicotine was self-administered or avoided. This study is important in that it points out the potential major role of environmental variables in modulating drug effects. Thus, instructions and expectations may also influence the abuse liability of NRTs.

Taking into account all of the studies that have examined the self-administration of nicotine versus placebo gum, it appears that nicotine gum functions at best as a weak reinforcer (i.e. active gum is sometimes, but not reliably, self-administered at greater rates than placebo gum). Therefore, based on this indicator, the abuse liability of nicotine gum is likely to be low.

## 4.3 Adverse Effects

Nicotine gum does not impair cognitive or psychomotor performance. In fact, the majority of studies that assessed performance during nicotine gum administration suggest that the gum enhances performance in abstaining smokers,[38] perhaps because it reduces the impairment associated with nicotine withdrawal.

A sizeable minority of users experience adverse effects from nicotine gum,[39] which may limit the likelihood of it being used excessively. The most common adverse effects include hiccups and gastrointestinal distress (stomach ache, nausea, vomiting).[39,40] Gum use *per se,* be it placebo or active, is also associated with complaints of jaw ache and mouth or throat soreness.[39,41]

## 4.4 Withdrawing Therapy and Epidemiology

There is some evidence that former cigarette smokers find it difficult to stop their use of nicotine gum. A meta-analysis of 10 studies reporting long term use of nicotine gum demonstrated that of those smokers who successfully abstained from cigarettes, 35% were still using the gum at 6 months and 20% were still using it at 1 year. Of successful abstainers, 35 to 90% were unable to stop using the gum at the recommended time.[42]

Another meta-analysis that examined long term use of nicotine gum compared with placebo gum in 315 medical patients found similar results (see fig. 2).[34] The study was conducted double-blind and patients were advised to quit gum chewing by 4 months. Nicotine gum administration was maintained for longer than the recommended period in a relatively high proportion of patients. This suggests that dependence, be it behavioural or physical, can develop with this NRT.

*In summary,* while some users of nicotine gum find it difficult to stop using the product, the large majority of smokers who use gum as an NRT do not do so for prolonged periods of time.[34] Relative to the difficulty in giving up cigarettes and the high relapse rate associated with abstinence from cigarettes, the nicotine gum has less abuse potential than cigarettes. Further, the subjective and reinforcing effects of nicotine gum as determined in laboratory studies are not suggestive of high abuse liability in either smokers or nonsmokers. Thus, nicotine gum has a relatively low potential for abuse compared with cigarettes.

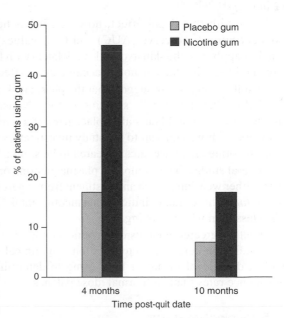

**Fig. 2.** Long term use of placebo and nicotine chewing gum in smokers attempting to quit. The figure shows the percentage of individuals (n = 315) in a placebo-controlled, double-blind trial who were still using placebo or nicotine gum at various time points after the quit date.[34]

## 5. Transdermal Nicotine Systems

### 5.1 Pharmacokinetics

The transdermal nicotine systems consist of an impermeable backing layer, a nicotine-containing reservoir, an adhesion layer and a removable protective layer. The method of nicotine delivery varies between systems that are currently available commercially.[43] In some systems, the nicotine is contained in a gel matrix or polymer form, and is in direct contact with the dermis. In other systems, nicotine delivery is controlled by a diffusion-controlling element that separates the reservoir from the skin.

The rate of nicotine delivery, besides being determined by the type of delivery system, is also affected by the intrinsic skin (stratum corneum) conductivity and degree of constriction of dermal blood vessels.[44] The nicotine dose is varied by altering the size of the patch.

The bioavailability of nicotine in a patch is 70 to 90%.[45,46] Like nicotine gum, the patch leads to slow absorption of nicotine into the venous system. Unlike nicotine absorbed from cigarettes, no plasma nicotine spikes occur (fig. 1). The onset of pharmacodynamic effects occurs within the first hour of placement of the patch.[45,46] Peak plasma concentration ($C_{max}$) of nicotine occurs within 7 to 9 hours of placement and then declines slowly over time.[46-48]

When the patch is removed, there is still a depot of nicotine in the skin that is slowly released over time.[47] This may partially account for why the terminal elimination half-life of nicotine is longer with the patch (4 to 5 hours) than with intravenous nicotine or smoked tobacco (2 hours).[45,46,48,49]

Even with this depot effect, however, it has been established that the area under the concentration-time curve (AUC) and $C_{max}$ values do not differ from the first day that a patch is applied to the skin to over 1 week later (with fresh patches being applied daily).[45,46,48] This indicates that there is not an accumulation effect from repeated administration.

Results from a study suggest that the pharmacokinetics of nicotine delivered via the patch depend on the individual's smoking history. Nonsmokers absorbed almost twice as much nicotine in the first 2 hours after placement of a 30mg patch, relative to a group of abstinent smokers.[50] It was unclear to the study investigators why absorption rates differed, especially since nicotine clearance rates appeared to be similar between the two groups.

Several studies have compared plasma nicotine or cotinine concentrations in smokers who were either wearing a patch and abstinent from cigarettes or not wearing the patch and smoking *ad libitum*. These studies indicate that nicotine intake while wearing the patch is approximately 40% less than while smoking.[51-53]

Whether greater amounts of nicotine should, therefore, be placed in the patch for heavily dependent smokers is open to question. No clinical study to date has tested nicotine patches with a dose level of higher than 21mg to determine if high-dose patches result in higher abstinence rates than do 'normal' dose patches.

### 5.2 Subjective Effects

Several clinical studies have examined the subjective effects of the transdermal nicotine patches in physically dependent smokers who abstained from smoking for some time before patch administration.

Placebo-controlled studies have documented that the nicotine patch reduced ratings of negative affective states such as irritability, anxiety, restlessness, difficulty concentrating and impatience in ex-smokers.[54-58] Unlike those assessing nicotine gum, these and other studies have documented that the patch also reduces craving for cigarettes.[59-61]

Two studies have assessed the subjective effects of the patch in smokers or nonsmokers under controlled laboratory conditions. In one study,[50] 8 life-long nonsmokers wore a 15 or 30mg patch and 8 abstinent smokers wore the 30mg patch for 24 hours. Whereas the smokers did not report any pleasant or unpleasant subjective effects from the patch, all 8 nonsmokers wearing the 30mg patch complained of negative subjective effects. These effects began within the first hour and included nausea and lightheadedness. Seven of the 8 nonsmokers dropped out of the study within 8 hours of patch placement due to these and other adverse effects (vomiting and headache). The majority of nonsmokers (5 of 8) who wore the 15mg patch also complained of negative symptomatology (e.g. nausea, vomiting, lightheadedness), but only 1 of these individuals dropped out of the study.

These findings suggested to the authors that the individuals in the smoking group were tolerant to the effects of nicotine, as they experienced little, if any, effect from the 30mg patch. However, this conclusion is confounded by the observation that the absorption rate of nicotine was twice as high in the nonsmoking compared to the smoking group. Thus, pharmacokinetic differences may have contributed to the differences between the groups.

In another study, the effects of high-dose patches were tested in light (n = 5) and heavy (n = 5) drug users who were also dependent smokers. Liking ratings did not vary with the dose of nicotine in the experimental patches (0, 30 or 60mg).[62] The authors concluded that the lack of liking indicated that the patch would have a low abuse liability in smokers.

## 5.3 Adverse Effects

We are aware of only two studies that have examined cognitive or psychomotor performance associated with use of the nicotine patch.

In one study,[62] smokers were allowed to smoke while wearing patches of different dose strengths, and there were no differences in psychomotor or cognitive performance across dosage conditions.

In the second study, smokers were not allowed to smoke while wearing the patches (dosage range 0 to 30 mg/16 hours). Nicotine abstinence slowed cognitive performance, and nicotine replacement via the patch attenuated the cognitive performance decrements.[63] Thus, there is little evidence that the nicotine patch influences psychomotor performance independent of its relief of withdrawal impairment.

Some users of the patch develop local mild skin irritation (itching and erythema) from the patch.[53,60,61] About 2 to 6% of patch users develop a severe allergic reaction at the site, necessitating discontinuation of the product.[3] A small proportion of patch users also report some nausea and vomiting, perhaps due to overdosage.[43,55]

## 5.4 Withdrawing Therapy and Epidemiology

Because the patch is a relatively new technology, data regarding the difficulty in withdrawal are not available. However, it has been speculated that stopping use of the patch may be relatively easy, because relatively few conditioned stimuli are associated with its use.[3] With other sources of nicotine, such as tobacco, gum, and the nasal spray (see section 6), stimuli such as sensorimotor cues, time of day and setting can provide conditioned cues that may promote use of the nicotine product and make it more difficult to stop its use. The patch, however, is placed on the body at the beginning of each day and produces a steady amount of nicotine in the systemic circulation, without distinctive conditioned stimuli. Consequently, the fact that the nicotine patch is not used on an 'as needed' basis, unlike nicotine gum, may make cessation of patch use easier than cessation of gum use.

*In summary*, the pharmacokinetics of the transdermal nicotine patch suggest that nicotine administered by this route is likely to have a lower abuse liability compared with smoking. This is because, when using the patch: (i) the onset of effect is slow and the nicotine 'spike' effect is absent; and (ii) the subjective effects are not strong. Two other factors that are likely to reduce the relative abuse liability of the patch are that there are fewer conditioned cues associated with its use compared with either cigarettes or nicotine gum, and the patch is not used on an 'as needed' basis.[3,43,64] Thus, the patch has a relatively low potential for abuse in comparison with cigarettes.

## 6. Nicotine Nasal Spray

Nicotine nasal spray is currently under consideration for approval by the US FDA for assisting in smoking cessation. Therefore, no clinical or epidemiological information regarding its actual abuse is available. However, limited laboratory data are available from the manufacturer (Kabi Pharmacia AB) and a from published source[20] on the pharmacokinetic and subjective aspects of this product relating to its abuse potential.

The pharmacokinetic profiles of nicotine nasal spray and inhaled tobacco smoke are similar in certain ways, but also differ in several important respects. Both methods of nicotine administration lead to a rapid increase in the venous concentrations of nicotine, which peak within 5 to 10 minutes (fig. 1).

However, one important difference is that inhaled tobacco smoke is absorbed into the arterial system, leading to very high arterial boluses of nicotine shortly after each puff,[65] whereas nicotine nasal spray is most likely to be absorbed into the venous system and therefore probably does not have this characteristic. The brief high arterial concentrations of drug attained through smoking are thought to account for the particularly addictive quality of drugs administered by smoking.[6] Drugs with a rapid onset of pharmacodynamic effect are believed to have a greater potential for abuse than drugs with a slower onset.[5,66]

Another difference in the kinetic profiles of nicotine nasal spray and cigarette smoke is that the therapeutic dose of nasal spray (2 sprays, each containing 0.5mg of nicotine) is lower than the dose of nicotine achieved from 1 cigarette.

Thus, although the pharmacokinetic profile of nicotine delivered via the nasal spray resembles more closely the pharmacokinetics of nicotine delivered by cigarettes than either the gum or the patch, there are also important differences in the kinetic profiles of the spray and cigarettes. These would be expected to result in the spray being less likely to be abused than cigarettes.

Using a different nasal spray method, Perkins et al.[67] directly compared the acute subjective effects of nicotine administered via tobacco smoking and nasal spray. They found that the plasma nicotine concentrations were similar across the two routes of administration, and that the pattern of subjective and physiological effects were also virtually identical. Under both conditions, individuals reported increased 'head rush' and dizziness and decreases in hunger and desire to smoke. Heart rate also increased under both conditions.

These findings suggest that, despite the high arterial nicotine concentrations known to occur with smoking but not with the nasal spray, the subjective effects of the two methods of administering nicotine were similar. Thus, this finding suggests that the abuse potential of the spray is likely to be similar to that of cigarettes.

One factor that may limit the likelihood of abuse of nicotine nasal spray is the relatively high incidence of adverse effects. Up to 90% of patients using nicotine nasal spray experience some adverse effects within the first 48 hours of use.[68] The most commonly reported effects include:

- nasal irritation
- runny nose
- sneezing
- throat irritation
- watering eyes
- coughing.

Despite the occurrence of these adverse effects, two clinical studies with cigarette smokers[20,68] indicate that a high proportion of patients continue to use, or even escalate their use of, the spray for extended periods of time.

Thus, the available data suggest that nicotine nasal spray is likely to have higher abuse potential than the nicotine gum or the nicotine patch, but it may nevertheless be less addictive than inhaled tobacco smoke.

## 7. Other Forms of Nicotine Replacement Therapy

Several other formulations for administration of nicotine have been developed, some of which have potential as NRTs. For example, lozenges containing nicotine are available as an over-the-counter aid to smoking cessation in England. A rudimentary pharmacokinetic study with these lozenges[69] indicated that nicotine absorption from 2 lozenges was similar to 1 piece of 2mg nicotine gum. Although a case report has been published that described a man who used these lozenges excessively,[69] not enough information is available about this product to evaluate its dependence liability.

The subjective and physiological effects of nicotine-containing toothpicks in cigarette smokers has been compared with those of nicotine gum.[70] The authors found that the total nicotine delivery and the cardiovascular and subjective effects of the two products were similar, but that nicotine was extracted more rapidly from the toothpicks than from the gum. This resulted in a two-fold higher plasma nicotine concentration 20 minutes after the beginning of chewing. To the extent that rapidity of onset is associated with increased likelihood of self-administration, these limited data would suggest that the dependence liability of toothpicks would be greater than that of the gum.

Jarvis et al.[71] have tested a nasal nicotine solution, administered as a droplet in the nose, as an NRT. They administered the solution (1 or 2mg strength) to 26 patients in a non–placebo-controlled trial. Although systematic pharmacokinetic data were not obtained, it may be assumed that absorption was comparable to that observed with the nasal spray. Most patients used the solution and found it helpful, in that it decreased their craving for cigarettes. Individuals reported some adverse effects, but these tended to decline over time. Several patients continued to use the solution for long periods of time (e.g. 12 months), raising the concern that there may be a high likelihood of continued use of the solution. However, this concern is difficult to evaluate because the investigators did not give patients any instructions about when to stop using the product.

The pharmacokinetic profile of inhaled aerosolised nicotine has also been examined.[72] The authors argue that NRTs that closely approximate the pharmacokinetics of smoking are likely to be most acceptable, and therefore most readily used, by cigarette smokers. They found that the rate of absorption of the aerosolised nicotine was comparable to that of smoked cigarettes, although higher doses of aerosolised nicotine were required to achieve the same $C_{max}$ as cigarettes (i.e. 5mg aerosol was equivalent to a 1 to 2mg cigarette). However, most of the individuals experienced unpleasant adverse effects from the aerosol, including coughing and burning sensations in the throat, and these effects were severe enough to cause almost one-half of the individuals who began the study to drop out.

Thus, although the pharmacokinetic profile of this formulation makes it likely that patients would use the product repeatedly (i.e. to self-administer), the adverse effects are likely to make it unacceptable to the majority of patients.

Finally, Leischow[73] reviewed experimental and clinical studies with a nicotine vaporiser, which may have potential as a NRT. The smoke-free vaporiser consists of a hollow plastic tube that contains a porous sponge permeated with nicotine. It delivers less nicotine per puff than a cigarette, and it results in a relatively slow time to $C_{max}$, similar to that of nicotine gum. Clinical studies with cigarette smokers indicate that the vaporiser may have potential as an aid to smoking cessation, although further safety and efficacy tests are needed.

## 8. Conclusion

This article has reviewed the pharmacokinetic and pharmacodynamic considerations and data relevant to the abuse liability of NRTs.

NRTs are important pharmacological adjuncts to the behavioural treatment of cigarette smoking. However, it is important to ensure that the products developed for treating nicotine dependence associated with cigarette smoking themselves have a low potential for abuse.

Based on the available evidence, it can be concluded that most of the NRTs have a low liability for abuse compared with tobacco cigarettes. Nevertheless, the various NRTs available and under development may differ in both the likelihood of repeated use (e.g. related to their rates of absorption and onset of pharmacodynamic effects) and the likelihood of adverse consequences (e.g. adverse effects).

Both of these factors may influence the abuse liability of NRTs and should be considered in future research into the development of new pharmacological aids to smoking cessation.

### Acknowledgements

Preparation of this manuscript was supported by the National Institute on Drug Abuse (DA02812) and the Clinical Practice Enhancement and Anaesthesia Research Foundation, with assistance from Matthew Clark.

### References

1.   Benowitz N. Pharmacologic aspects of cigarette smoking and nicotine addiction. N Engl J Med 1988; 319: 1318-30
2.   Stolerman IP, Jarvis MJ. The scientific case that nicotine is addictive. Psychopharmacology 1995; 117: 2-10
3.   Hughes J. Risk-benefit assessment of nicotine preparations in smoking cessation. Drug Saf 1993; 8: 49-56
4.   Busto U, Sellers E. Pharmacokinetic determinants of drug abuse and dependence. Clin Pharmacokinet 1986; 11: 144-53

5.  de Wit H, Dudish S, Ambre J. Subjective and behavioral effects of diazepam depend on its rate of onset. Psychopharmacology 1993; 112: 324-30
6.  Henningfield J, Keenan R. Nicotine delivery kinetics and abuse liability. J Consult Clin Psychol 1993; 61: 1-8
7.  American Psychiatric Association. Diagnostic and statistical manual of mental disorders. 4th ed. Washington, DC: American Psychiatric Association, 1994
8.  Jasinski DR. History of abuse liability testing in humans. Br J Addict 1991; 86: 1559-62
9.  McNair D, Lorr M, Droppleman L. Profile of mood states [manual]. San Diego: Educational and Industrial Testing Service, 1971
10. Martin W, Sloan J, Sapira J, et al. Physiological, subjective and behavioral effects of amphetamine, methamphetamine, ephedrine, phenmetrazine and methylphenidate in man. Clin Pharmacol Ther 1971; 12: 245-58
11. Hindmarch I. Psychomotor function and psychoactive drugs. Br J Clin Pharmacol 1980; 10: 189-209
12. Foltin RW, Evans SM. Performance effects of drugs of abuse. Hum Psychopharmacol 1993; 8: 9-19
13. Henningfield J, Goldberg S. Cigarette smokers self-administer intravenous nicotine. Pharmacol Biochem Behav 1983; 19: 887-90
14. Pomerleau C, Pomerleau O. Euphoriant effects of nicotine in smokers. Psychopharmacology 1992; 108: 460-5
15. Foltin R, Fischman M. Assessment of abuse liability of stimulant drugs in humans: a methodological survey. Drug Alcohol Depend 1991; 28: 3-48
16. de Wit H, Griffiths RR. Testing the abuse liability of anxiolytic and hypnotic drugs in humans. Drug Alcohol Depend 1991; 28: 83-111
17. Benowitz N, Jacob P, Savanapridi C. Determinants of nicotine intake while chewing nicotine polacrilex gum. Clin Pharmacol Ther 1987; 41: 467-73
18. Svensson CK. Clinical pharmacokinetics of nicotine. Clin Pharmacokinet 1987; 12: 30-40
19. Benowitz N, Porchet H, Shelner L, et al. Nicotine absorption and cardiovascular effects with smokeless tobacco use: comparison with cigarettes and nicotine gum. Clin Pharmacol Ther 1988; 44 (1): 23-8
20. Sutherland G, Russell M, Stapleton J, et al. Nasal nicotine spray: a rapid nicotine delivery system. Psychopharmacology 1992; 108: 512-8
21. Jarvis M, Raw M, Russell M, et al. Randomized control trial of nicotine chewing gum. BMJ 1982; 285: 537-40
22. Hughes J, Hatsukami D, Pickens R, et al. Effect of nicotine on the tobacco withdrawal syndrome. Psychopharmacology 1984; 83: 82-7
23. Schneider N, Jarvik M, Forsythe A. Nicotine vs. placebo gum in the alleviation of withdrawal during smoking cessation. Addict Behav 1984; 9: 149-56
24. West R, Jarvis M, Russell M, et al. Effect of nicotine replacement on the cigarette withdrawal syndrome. Br J Addict 1984; 79: 215-9
25. Heishman S, Snyder F, Henningfield J. Performance, subjective, and physiological effects of nicotine in non-smokers. Drug Alcohol Depend 1993; 34: 11-8
26. Haertzen C. Development of scales based on patterns of drug effects using the Addiction Research Center Inventory (ARCI). Psychol Rep 1966; 18: 163-94
27. Jasinski D, Martin W, Sapira J. Antagonism of the subjective, behavioral, pupillary, and respiratory depressant effects of cyclazocine by naloxone. Clin Pharmacol Ther 1968; 9: 215-22
28. Coslett-Nemeth R, Benowitz N, Robinson N, et al. Nicotine gum: chew rate, subjective effects and plasma nicotine. Pharmacol Biochem Behav 1988; 29: 747-51
29. Pickworth W, Herning R, Henningfield J. Electroencephalographic effects of nicotine chewing gum in humans. Pharmacol Biochem Behav 1986; 25: 879-82
30. Wewers M, Tejwani G, Anderson J. Plasma nicotine, plasma beta-endorphin and mood states during periods of chronic smoking, abstinence and nicotine replacement. Psychopharmacology 1994; 116: 98-102
31. Shiffman S, Jarvik M. Smoking withdrawal. Symptoms in two weeks of abstinence. Psychopharmacology 1976; 50: 35-9
32. Gross J, Stitzer M. Nicotine replacement: ten-week effects on tobacco withdrawal symptoms. Psychopharmacology 1989; 98: 334-41
33. West R, Schneider N. Craving for cigarettes. Br J Addict 1985; 82: 407-15
34. Hughes J, Gust S, Keenan R, et al. Long-term use of nicotine vs placebo gum. Arch Intern Med 1991; 151: 1993-8
35. Hughes J, Strickler G, King D, et al. Smoking history, instructions and the effects of nicotine: two pilot studies. Pharmacol Biochem Behav 1989; 34: 149-55
36. Hughes J, Pickens R, Spring W, et al. Instructions control whether nicotine will serve as a reinforcer. J Pharmacol Exp Ther 1985; 235: 106-12
37. Hughes J, Gulliver S, Amoria G, et al. Effect of instructions and nicotine on smoking cessation, withdrawal symptoms and self-administration of nicotine gum. Psychopharmacology 1989; 99: 486-91
38. Sherwood N. Effects of nicotine on human psychomotor performance. Hum Psychopharmacol 1993; 8: 155-84
39. Hughes J, Gust S, Keenan R, et al. Nicotine vs placebo gum in general medical practice. JAMA 1989; 261: 1300-5
40. Hughes J, Miller S. Nicotine gum to help stop smoking. JAMA 1984; 252: 2855-8
41. Schneider N, Jarvik M, Forsythe A, et al. Nicotine gum in smoking cessation: a placebo-controlled, double-blind trial. Addict Beh 1983; 8: 253-61
42. Hughes J. Long term use of nicotine replacement therapy. In: Henningfield J, Stitzer M, editors. New developments in nicotine delivery systems: proceedings of a conference; 1990 Sept 24: Johns Hopkins University. Ossining (NY): Cortlandt Communications, 1991
43. Palmer KJ, Buckley MM, Faulds D. Transdermal nicotine: a review of its pharmacodynamic and pharmacokinetic properties, and therapeutic efficacy as an aid to smoking cessation. Drugs 1992; 44: 498-529

44. Benowitz N, Jacob P, Olsson P, et al. Intravenous nicotine retards transdermal absorption of nicotine: evidence of blood flow-limited percutaneous absorption. Clin Pharmacol Ther 1992; 52: 223-30
45. Bannon Y, Corish J, Corrigan O, et al. Transdermal delivery of nicotine in normal human volunteers: a single dose and multiple dose study. Eur J Clin Pharmacol 1989; 37: 285-90
46. Gupta S, Benowitz N, Jacob P, et al. Bioavailability and absorption kinetics of nicotine following application of a transdermal system. Br J Clin Pharmacol 1993; 36: 221-7
47. Dubois J, Sioufi A, Muller P, et al. Pharmacokinetics and bioavailability of nicotine in healthy volunteers following single and repeated administration of different doses of transdermal nicotine systems. Methods Find Exp Clin Pharmacol 1989; 11: 187-95
48. Caspary S, Keller-Stanislawski B, Huber T, et al. Pharmacokinetics of nicotine after application of a 30 cm$^2$ nicotine patch under steady-state conditions. Int J Clin Psychopharmacol 1991; 29: 92-5
49. Kochak G, Sun J, Choi R, et al. Pharmacokinetic disposition of multiple-dose transdermal nicotine in healthy adult smokers. Pharm Res 1992; 9: 1451-5
50. Srivastava E, Russell M, Feyerabend C, et al. Sensitivity and tolerance to nicotine in smokers and nonsmokers. Psychopharmacology 1991; 105: 63-8
51. Daughton D, Heatley S, Prendergast J. Effect of transdermal nicotine delivery as an adjunct to low-intervention smoking cessation therapy – a randomized double-blind placebo-controlled trial. Mayo Clin Proc 1991; 65: 1529-37
52. Tonnesen P, Norregaard J, Simonsen K, et al. A double-blind trial of a 16-hour transdermal nicotine patch in smoking cessation. N Engl J Med 1991; 325: 311-5
53. Hurt R, Dale L, Offord K, et al. Serum nicotine and cotinine levels during nicotine-patch therapy. Clin Pharmacol Ther 1993; 54: 98-106
54. Rose J, Levin E, Behm F, et al. Transdermal nicotine facilitates smoking cessation. Clin Pharmacol Ther 1990; 47: 323-30
55. Group TNS. Transdermal nicotine for smoking cessation: six-month results from two multicenter controlled clinical trials. JAMA 1991; 266: 3133-8
56. Group ICRFGPR. Effectiveness of a nicotine patch in helping people to stop smoking: results of a randomized trial in general practice. BMJ 1993; 306: 1304-8
57. Russell M, Stapleton J, Feyerabend C, et al. Targeting heavy smokers in general practice: randomized controlled trial of transdermal nicotine patches. BMJ 1993; 306: 1308-12
58. Fagerstrom K, Schneider N, Lunell E. Effectiveness of nicotine patch and nicotine gum as individual versus combined treatments for tobacco withdrawal symptoms. Psychopharmacology 1993; 111: 271-7
59. Abelin T, Ehrsam R, Buhler-Reichert A, et al. Effectiveness of a transdermal nicotine system in smoking cessation studies. Methods Find Exp Clin Pharmacol 1989; 11: 205-14
60. Muller P, Abelin T, Ehrsam R, et al. The use of transdermal nicotine in smoking cessation. Lung Supp 1990; 1: 445-3
61. Levin E, Westman E, Stein R, et al. Nicotine skin patch treatment increases abstinence, decreases withdrawal symptoms, and attenuates rewarding effects of smoking. J Clin Psychopharmacol 1994; 14: 41-9
62. Bunker E, Pickworth W, Henningfield J. Nicotine patch: effect on spontaneous smoking. In: Harris L, editor. National Institute on Drug Abuse research monograph series 119, problems of drug dependence 1991. Rockville (MD): USPHS, 1992
63. Pickworth WB, Butschky MF, Henningfield JE. A nicotine patch reduces subjective and objective measures of tobacco withdrawal. In: Harris L, editor. National Institute on Drug Abuse research monograph series 153. Rockville (MD): USPHS, 1995: 194
64. Schneider N. Nicotine therapy in smoking cessation: pharmacokinetic considerations. Clin Pharmacokinet 1992; 23: 169-72
65. Henningfield J, London E, Benowitz N. Arterial-venous differences in plasma concentrations of nicotine after cigarette smoking. JAMA 1990; 263: 2049-50
66. Jaffe J. Drug addiction and drug abuse. In: Gilman A, Raul T, Nies A, et al., editors. The pharmacological basis of therapeutics. New York: Pergamon Press, 1990: 522-73
67. Perkins KA, Sexton J, Reynolds W, et al. Comparison of acute subjective and heart rate effects of nicotine intake via tobacco smoking versus nasal spray. Pharmacol Biochem Behav 1994; 47: 295-9
68. Hjalmarson A, Franzon M, Westin A, et al. Effect of nicotine nasal spray on smoking cessation. Arch Intern Med 1994; 154: 2567-72
69. Belcher M, Jarvis M, Sutherland G. Nicotine absorption and dependence in an over the counter aid to stopping smoking. BMJ 1989; 298: 570
70. Hasenfratz M, Battig K. Nicotine absorption and the subjective and physiologic effects of nicotine toothpicks. Clin Pharmacol Ther 1991; 50: 456-61
71. Jarvis M, Hajek P, Russell M, et al. Nasal nicotine solution as an aid to cigarette withdrawal: a pilot clinical trial. Br J Addict 1987; 82: 983-8
72. Burch S, Erbland M, Gann L, et al. Plasma nicotine levels after inhalation of aerosolized nicotine. Am Rev Respir Dis 1989; 140: 955-7
73. Leischow SJ. The nicotine vaporizer. Health Values 1994; 18: 4-9

---

Correspondence: Dr *Harriet de Wit*, Department of Psychiatry, The University of Chicago, 5841 S. Maryland Avenue, Chicago, IL 60637, USA.

# Cost Effectiveness of Smoking-Cessation Therapies

## Interpretation of the Evidence and Implications for Coverage

*Kenneth E. Warner*

Department of Health Management and Policy, School of Public Health, University of
Michigan, Michigan, USA

The advent of pharmacological nicotine replacement therapy (NRT) in the 1980s fundamentally altered the smoking-cessation treatment landscape. Before the availability of NRT,
counselling and behavioural conditioning constituted the principal techniques used by professionals to treat patients with nicotine addiction, although a myriad of other approaches existed
as well, including self-help manuals, hypnosis, acupuncture, and devices such as progressive
filtration systems. As these approaches suggest, much (perhaps most) of the formal attempts
to treat nicotine addiction took place outside the conventional medical care system.

The significance of the introduction of NRT was 2-fold. First, it provided clinicians with a
pharmacological intervention that was documented to significantly increase cessation rates.[1]
Second, by doing so, it effectively 'medicalised' the treatment of nicotine addiction. No longer
restricted to a counselling function, for which they were not well trained (and often not re-
imbursed), clinicians could write prescriptions for their smoking patients. Patients could leave
clinical visits with something more than an embarrassing exhortation to quit. For both parties,
the prescription lent the patient-provider interaction the desired aura of conventional medical
care. This undoubtedly increased counselling by providers, along with the writing of prescriptions. The counselling alone would be expected to at least double the average smoker's chance
of quitting in a given year.[1,2]

Cost-effectiveness analyses (CEAs) of a variety of approaches to smoking cessation, including the use of NRT,[3,4] have shown the validity of Eddy's conclusion[5] that smoking
cessation is the 'gold standard' of healthcare cost effectiveness. All of the smoking interventions studied saved life-years at costs ranging from a few hundred to a few thousand US dollars.
These figures fall well below those estimated for the vast majority of the evaluated primary-,
secondary- and tertiary-care medical interventions that are covered by healthcare providers and
insurers. However, treatment of smoking cessation is often not covered by these same providers
and insurers. Taken at face value, there appears to be a serious contradiction between this fact
and the cost-effectiveness evidence.

After identifying the principal findings from the CEA literature concerning smoking
cessation, this article considers important subtleties in how these findings should be interpreted. Attention then turns to the implications of the cost effectiveness of smoking cessation

with regard to whether or not providers and insurers should cover the costs of treatment, and, if so, which treatments ought to be covered. This discussion also considers other factors that influence whether or not providers and insurers choose to cover such services. The article concludes with observations on the limitations and overall utility of CEA, deriving lessons that pertain to the analysis and financing of preventive services in general, as well as smoking cessation in particular.

## 1. Principal Findings from Cost-Effectiveness Analyses

Although the literature on the cost effectiveness of smoking cessation is not extensive, it includes studies that cover a range of smoking-cessation interventions for individual smokers, from the least resource-intensive (e.g. distribution of self-help cessation guides by non-physician personnel,[6,7] quit contests[6,8,9]), to those that are, in relative terms, resource-intensive (e.g. physician counselling,[10] and the use of NRT products as adjuncts to physician advice to quit[3,4]). The most resource-intensive interventions, such as substantial physician counselling on both quitting and maintenance, combined with use of NRT, have not been subjected to CEA.

Typically, the CEAs have evaluated interventions on the basis of their efficiency (cost effectiveness) in producing smoking cessation, measured in terms of cost per quitter, and in avoiding premature deaths, measured as cost per life-year saved. A few cost-benefit analyses (CBAs) are also to be found in this literature, the majority of which have focused on smoking-cessation interventions during pregnancy.[11-14] Although traditional healthcare CBAs include the valuation of life-saving *per se* in assessing the monetary value of all costs and benefits,[15] the emphasis within the smoking-cessation literature is on the savings in healthcare expenditures resulting from the avoidance of smoking.[16,17] As such, several of the smoking-cessation 'CBAs' might more properly be labelled cost-savings analyses, although they will be referred to in this article as CBAs, consistent with their authors' designation of them.

The pregnancy-related studies lend themselves to CBA because of the relative ease of estimating the principal monetary benefit associated with quitting, namely the avoidance of additional hospitalisation costs in neonatal intensive care units. In contrast, most of the CEA literature examines cessation programmes in the general adult population.

Table I shows the major characteristics of, and findings from, CEAs on a variety of smoking-cessation interventions. Table II shows the same for CBAs. In the remainder of this article, however, attention will focus exclusively on the CEAs.

The CEA literature on smoking cessation is plagued by problems that permeate CEAs more generally, ranging from inadequacies in controls to cost-measurement problems. Elixhauser[21] has described the problems found in the smoking-cessation literature published through the 1980s; the limitations of applying CEA in the pharmaceutical arena have been recently reviewed,[22-24] as have the general issues and concerns relating to both CBA and CEA.[15,25]

Although important differences in methods and measures make comparisons across studies imprecise, the literature yields consistent patterns of findings that permit two important generalisations concerning the cost effectiveness of smoking-cessation interventions. The first (section 1.1) is the more intriguing, deserving careful interpretation (which it receives in section 2), while the second is the more important (section 1.2).

## 1.1 Costs Rise Faster Than Effectiveness

On average, the cost per life-year saved appears to rise as the resource intensity of the intervention rises. The least intensive interventions, such as distribution of self-help cessation manuals and brief counselling by nonphysician health professionals, result in smoking cessation at a cost of only a few hundred US dollars per quitter,[6,7] suggesting a cost per life-year

**Table I.** Characteristics of and findings from cost-effectiveness analyses of smoking cessation. All of the resulting estimates are rounded to 2 significant figures. Readers are cautioned that this inflation adjustment process is necessarily imprecise, as it cannot capture price changes specific to the resources used in each intervention

| Population studied | Type of intervention | Method | Effectiveness measure | Costs (1995 values)[a] |
|---|---|---|---|---|
| Hypothetical adult medical patients[3] | Nicotine gum as adjunct to physician counselling | Estimates from literature | Cost per life-year saved | Men: $US8500-$US13 000 Women: $US14 000-$US20 000 |
| Hypothetical adult medical patients[4] | Nicotine patch as adjunct to physician counselling | Decision analysis based on estimates from literature | Cost per additional quitter | $US7300 |
| | | | Cost per quality-adjusted life year saved | Men: $US4400-$US11 000 Women: $US5000-$US8000 |
| Community volunteers[6] | 1. Cessation class 2. Contest 3. Self-help kit | Evaluation of community programmes | Cost per quitter (after 1 year and after 5 years) | 1. $US670 and $US470 2. $US500 and $US260 3. $US240 and $US84 |
| Pregnant women in PH maternity clinics[7] | 1. Standard information and advice 2. No. 1 + standard self-help manual 3. No. 1 + pregnancy self-help manual | Randomised trial | Cost per quitter | 1. $US190 2. $US220 3. $US92 |
| Adults (≥16 years) in Sweden[8] | Mass media quit contest plus county-level organisational strategy | Quasi-experiment | Cost per life-year saved | $US1400-$US1600 |
| Adults (≥16 years) in Sweden[9] | 1. Mass media 2. Mass media plus county-level organisational strategy | Quasi-experiment | Cost per quitter | 1. $US290 2. $US250 |
| Hypothetical adult medical patients[10] | Physician counselling | Estimates from literature | Cost per life-year saved | Men: $US1500-$US2100 Women: $US2500-$US4300 |
| Pregnant women[12] | Nonphysician counselling, instructional materials and follow-up phone calls | Estimates from literature | Cost per low birthweight birth averted | $US6400 |
| | | | Cost per perinatal death averted | $US110 000 |
| Patients after acute myocardial infarction[18] | Nurse-managed cessation counselling | Model based on effectiveness data | Cost per life-year saved | $US300 |
| Hypothetical blue-collar workers[19] | Hypothetical worksite smoking cessation programme | Computer simulation based on estimates from literature | Cost per quitter Cost per life-year saved | $US1500 $US900 |

a   Costs presented in the original studies in earlier years' US dollars were adjusted to 1995 US dollars using the Consumer Price Index (CPI) and/or its medical care component, the Medical Care Price Index (MCPI): for interventions that were primarily medical, only the MCPI was used; for interventions that took place outside of the medical system (e.g. community interventions), only the CPI was used; for interventions that had significant medical and nonmedical components (e.g. medical clinic interventions that relied heavily on self-help guides), an equally-weighted mix of the CPI and the MCPI was used.

**PH** = public health.

**Table II.** Characteristics of and findings from cost-benefit analyses on smoking cessation. All of the resulting estimates are rounded to 2 significant figures

| Population studied | Type of intervention | Method | Findings |
|---|---|---|---|
| Pregnant women in an HMO[11] | Mailed self-help materials, in addition to usual care | Randomised trial | Benefit-cost ratio: 2.8 : 1 |
| Pregnant women[12] | Nonphysician counselling, instructional materials and follow-up phone calls | Estimates from literature | Benefit-cost ratio, net savings in neonatal intensive-care unit hospitalisation costs: 3.3 : 1<br>Benefit-cost ratio, including avoidance of long-term care costs: 6.6 : 1 |
| Pregnant women in PH maternity clinics[13] | Nonphysician counselling, self-help cessation booklet, follow-up counselling and 'buddy' programme | Randomised trial | Benefit-cost ratio: 6.7 : 1 to 17.2 : 1 |
| Pregnant women[14]a | Hypothetical 'average' intervention | Decision-tree analysis | Break-even cost: programme cost beneficial if programme cost $US86 (1995 value), assuming cessation rate of 18% |
| Hypothetical workers[19] | Multiple smoking-cessation interventions | Decision-tree analysis | Greatest benefit from nicotine patch with pharmacist consultation and to patient participation in formal cessation programme |
| Hypothetical blue-collar workers[20] | Hypothetical worksite smoking cessation programme | Computer simulation based on estimates from literature | Benefit-cost ratio: 8.8 : 1 |

a  Was referred to as a cost-effectiveness analysis, but was in fact a cost-benefit analysis.

**HMO** = health maintenance organisation; **PH** = public health.

saved of less than $US1000. In contrast, brief advice by physicians raises the cost to a few thousand US dollars,[10] while the use of nicotine gum or patches as an adjunct to physician advice increases the cost to as much as $US10 000 to $US20 000 per life-year saved.[3,4]

Table I does not show, for each intervention, the breakdown of the costs and effectiveness that comprise the numerator and denominator, respectively, of the cost-effectiveness ratio. The composition of cost-effectiveness ratios may be critically important in understanding the relative merits of the different interventions (section 2).

The important point is that the more resource-intensive interventions are typically more effective than the less-intensive interventions, but the costs of the former are proportionately even higher than those of the latter. In other words, as the resource intensity of the intervention rises, both costs and effectiveness increase, but costs increase more rapidly than effectiveness. Thus, the more effective interventions have what appear on the surface to be less attractive cost-effectiveness ratios. As is discussed in section 2, however, these findings should not be interpreted as implying (as they seem to do at face value) that the least intensive interventions are necessarily always superior and preferred to the most intensive.[1]

## 1.2 Cessation is Highly Cost Effective in Relative Terms

Across all of the interventions, smoking cessation emerges as a highly cost-effective healthcare expenditure. The interventions that are in the low-to-medium range for cost per life-year saved in table I are similar to, or better than, the cost per life-year saved found among the most effective primary-prevention healthcare practices.[26] Even the use of nicotine gum as an adjunct to physician counselling – the intervention that saves lives at the highest cost of those included in table I[3] – compares very favourably with other widely practised prevention interventions.

Frequently cited examples of comparable interventions are the treatment of mild and moderate hypertension ($US51 000 and $US24 000 per life-year saved, respectively) and the treatment of hypercholesterolaemia (serum cholesterol level ≥6.85 mmol/L) with cholestyramine ($US136 000 to $US224 000 per life-year saved) [values adjusted to 1995 dollars].[10] Evaluating nearly 600 life-saving interventions that included injury control and toxin-reduction strategies, in addition to medical practices, a group of researchers recently concluded that the median intervention cost is $US42 000 per life-year saved (1993 values), with many widely practised interventions, both medical and nonmedical, costing well in excess of $US100 000 per life-year saved.[26]

## 2. Interpreting the Cost-Effectiveness Evidence

In order to interpret these findings carefully, it is important to understand the correct meaning of the term 'cost effective'. The literature suggests that many healthcare professionals who use the term do not possess this understanding. The term has been used quite loosely (and frequently inappropriately) in the literature, to refer to interventions that are deemed by the writer to be either effective or inexpensive, without regard to the other characteristic. The comparative perspective, discussed in the next paragraph, has often been missing completely.[27]

Technically, 'cost effective' is a comparative term: a given intervention is deemed to be cost effective if: (i) it achieves a given quantified objective at a lower cost than all alternative interventions intended to achieve the same objective; or (ii) it achieves more of the desired objective than do the alternatives when identical levels of resources are devoted to each intervention.[15]

In practice, many CEAs lack an internal direct comparative perspective. Rather, the drug, procedure or technology being evaluated is compared, either explicitly or implicitly, with some exogenous standard of what constitutes cost-effective care. Examples include prominent CEAs of physician counselling,[10] and of the use of NRT products as an adjunct to physician counselling.[3,4] In both situations, the cost per life-year saved for the intervention was compared with estimates of cost per life-year saved for other kinds of medical treatments for other disease problems, found elsewhere in the healthcare literature. Similarly, in section 1.2 of this article, the conclusion was drawn that the full range of evaluated smoking-cessation treatments constitutes cost-effective care because all of the interventions save life-years at a lower cost than commonly accepted primary-, secondary- and tertiary-care procedures.

### 2.1 Low-Intensity versus High-Intensity Interventions

Elements of the appropriate comparative perspective in CEAs are quite subtle, and are well illustrated by the analyses of smoking-cessation interventions. As noted in section 1.1, that literature clearly suggests that the low-intensity (or 'low-tech') interventions save life-years at less cost than the more resource-intensive (or 'high-tech') interventions. Does this mean that low-tech interventions should be used extensively, while high-intensity interventions should be abandoned, with all treatment resources dedicated to the low-tech approaches? If so, this would effectively rule out use of NRT.

The answer is a distinct 'no' for at least three reasons. The first is that comparison of cost-effectiveness ratios *per se* is technically invalid when neither cost nor effectiveness is held constant across studies. Decisions based on direct comparisons of such ratios can lead to undesirable results, as will be demonstrated in section 2.1.1. Second, different approaches to smoking cessation may be more or less effective (and cost effective) for different groups of people. This is rarely acknowledged in the CEA literature, and almost not at all in smoking-cessation CEAs (although it is discussed in the effectiveness literature).[1] Third, cost-effectiveness information should be used not only within the category of smoking-cessation interventions (where it is certainly appropriate), but also across different categories of healthcare interventions, as was done in section 1.2.

### 2.1.1 Lack of Constancy of Costs or Effectiveness

Reliance on the bottom-line measure of a CEA, the cost-effectiveness ratio, to determine the relative preference for competing interventions can lead to an undesirable allocation of resources, unless either the costs or outcomes sought are the same among the interventions being compared.

Suppose that Intervention A saves 10 life-years at a total cost of $US10 000, implying a cost-effectiveness ratio of $US1000 per life-year saved, and that Intervention B saves 20 life-years at a cost of $US25 000, or $US1250 per life-year saved. If one defines preference solely on the basis of the cost-effectiveness ratio, A would be clearly superior to B. However, consider the true comparative virtues of the 2 interventions. B saves 10 more life-years for an extra $US15 000, or $US1500 for each extra life-year. Surely this is a sensational buy: who would argue that a year of life saved is not worth $US1500? If Interventions A and B could not be replicated, from a social perspective, B would clearly dominate A, despite the former having a less attractive ratio of costs to effectiveness. Only if A could be replicated, with the same relative costs and effectiveness, would it clearly dominate B, since 2 'units' of A would then save the same 20 life-years as B at a total cost $5000 less than B. This emphasises the need for caution in interpreting cost-effectiveness ratios at face value, without considering what underlies their numerators and denominators.

### 2.1.2 Costs and Effectiveness Vary by Types of Smokers

It is plausible that people who successfully quit smoking while using high-intensity interventions, such as physician counselling with NRT, may not be susceptible, or may be substantially less susceptible, to the low-intensity interventions, such as self-help guides. If this is true, for this group of smokers, the counselling-NRT combination may be considerably more cost effective than the self-help guide, simply because the latter is not effective for them. The literature does not permit appreciation of this distinction, since CEAs comparing categorically different types of interventions are essentially nonexistent. Randomised controlled trials have generated effectiveness data primarily (although not exclusively) in the area of NRT, in which the only 'alternative' intervention is placebo.

If, as seems likely, different types of smokers respond differently to different kinds of interventions, the argument for supporting all cost-effective smoking-cessation interventions is strengthened. Although the science is in its infancy, progress is being made in developing the ability to distinguish which smokers are most suitable for which types of interventions.[1] If that ability is ever refined to the point of some precision, we will be able to define which interventions are cost effective for which smokers. Until that time, we should be providing a range of options to smokers who want to quit, so long as each included option is generally regarded as cost effective in saving lives compared with other widely practised medical and health procedures. As indicated in section 1.2, all of the mainstream interventions evaluated to date fall into this category.

### 2.1.3 Use of Cost-Effectiveness Data Across Categories

The third concern about uncritical interpretation of cost-effectiveness ratios is that comparisons should occur across categories of interventions, as well as within them. In the smoking-cessation CEA literature, the important message is not that 'low-tech' approaches are superior to 'high-tech' interventions (as a result of the former's lower cost-effectiveness ratios), but rather that *all* of the studied interventions are healthcare bargains; a life-year saved at a cost of less than $US20 000 (the highest cost estimate found in the smoking-cessation treatment literature) constitutes a very worthwhile investment.

### 2.2 Factors not Considered in the Literature

In discussing the proper interpretation of the CEA evidence, it is important to note certain omissions from the relevant literature. Some omissions are inevitable, reflecting the problem of keeping up with rapid changes in both the technological and social modes of delivering NRTs. Their inevitability notwithstanding, these omissions make the existing literature at least partially out of date.

With regard to technology, newly emerging NRT technologies, notably the inhaler and the nasal spray, have not been subjected to cost-effectiveness analysis, in part because the determination of basic efficacy is too new. Although the nicotine patch has been marketed for several years now, the first study evaluating its cost effectiveness was only published in 1996.[4]

With regard to the social mode of delivery, over-the-counter (OTC) availability of NRT products that previously were available exclusively by prescription fundamentally alters the cost-effectiveness equation for both prescription and OTC NRT. Although other countries have had nonprescription NRT products for quite a while, nicotine gum and patches became available over the counter in the US only in 1996.

As a consequence of this shift in the regulation of availability, both the costs and effectiveness of NRT, as conventionally understood, are likely to change, possibly substantially. OTC use of gum or patches, without professional counselling, is almost certain to yield a lower rate of success in quitting smoking; at the same time, however, the cost of an attempt will be considerably lower as well, as a result of both the lower price of the OTC product, compared with that available by prescription, and the absence of professional charges. (According to one recent study,[28] however, smokers' demand for OTC NRT may be quite price sensitive, at least for young smokers.)

Will OTC NRT be more or less cost effective than prescription NRT (with counselling)? The changing mode of availability may cause profound shifts in who tries to quit, how often, and with what success. OTC availability seems very likely to reduce the number of people who receive professional counselling along with an NRT product, but it is also likely to considerably expand the number of people who try to quit with such products. Those who would have consulted their physicians in the absence of OTC availability, but choose to 'go it alone' with an OTC NRT product, are likely to have a lower quit rate. Those who would not have consulted physicians, but will try the OTC NRT product on their own, will probably have a higher quit rate.

One group of researchers[29] has modelled the possibilities and concluded that OTC availability of nicotine gum is more likely than not to increase the net amount of people quitting smoking in the US; their most likely estimate is that 450 000 more people in the US will be abstinent by the end of 10 years as a consequence of OTC availability.[29] Should this prove to be the result, the move to OTC availability will itself probably rank as a cost-effective innovation in the treatment of nicotine dependence. Of course, the opposite is possible as well: use of OTC gum (or patches) without counselling may have little marginal benefit over quitting attempts without either counselling or NRT. Unsuccessful quitters may become more resigned to their fate and hence resistant to future counselling efforts by their physicians. If this is the result, OTC NRT may prove to be highly cost ineffective.

One final category of omitted approaches to smoking cessation warrants mention here. Although the CEA literature covers the spectrum of patient-provider interventions, it has to date included very few examples of the smoking-cessation interventions that are the least resource-intensive, relative to the population reached: the collective social measures and policies that are often labelled 'public health interventions'.

A notable example is the broadcast media anti-smoking campaign. Both at the national level and in individual states in the US and elsewhere, media campaigns to encourage cessation have been documented to have reduced smoking by significant amounts.[30,31] Many knowledgeable observers believe that such interventions may save life-years at extraordinarily low costs relative to one-on-one patient-provider interactions,[30,32] although the cost-effectiveness evidence on this point is limited, with the handful of relevant studies having focused on the cost per quitter,[9,33] rather than the cost per life-year saved.[8] Appealing to simple cost-effectiveness logic, one prominent tobacco-and-health scholar concluded that one-on-one interventions ought to be abandoned in their entirety, with the resources devoted instead to developing a substantial and sustained anti-smoking media campaign.[32] For a given total expenditure, the media campaign would cause many more people to quit smoking. Although the one-on-one interventions were more effective, their cost per quitter was dramatically higher.[32]

However compelling this argument might seem at first blush, it fails for precisely the same reasons that we should not reject the more expensive one-on-one interventions simply because the 'low-tech' treatment options have more attractive cost-effectiveness ratios (section 2.1). In this instance,[32] the failure of the argument is even stronger, since it is unlikely that funding for the collective and individual interventions is derived from the same source and, hence, that public and personal interventions are necessarily 'competing'. On the contrary, they may be highly complementary, with public measures altering the social environment in a manner conducive to more individuals seeking help with quitting, and more being successful.[34] This potential to reduce smoking – both directly and indirectly, the latter through synergistic effects with individual treatment interventions – suggests that researchers should undertake formal CEAs of public health measures.

## 3. Coverage of Cost-Effective Interventions by Providers and Insurers

Should cost-effective interventions be covered by healthcare providers and insurers? Given the CEA evidence, it might be suspected that the only logical response to this question would be a strong and unequivocal affirmative. An affirmative judgment does seem warranted, although as is discussed in this section, the case is much less clear-cut than might be expected.

Ultimately, support for coverage derives from the related criteria that the healthcare system should support cost-effective care and that most healthcare systems currently cover a wide range of procedures that are demonstrably less cost-effective than the treatment of smoking cessation. If smoking-cessation therapy is not covered, the system will encourage less cost-effective alternatives that are covered (up to and including treatment of smoking-induced lung cancer). The system encourages use of these alternatives both directly, through the economic incentive afforded by coverage, and indirectly, through the implicit message (sent to consumers) that smoking-cessation therapy must not be 'worth it' if the system does not deem it worthy of coverage.

Despite this endorsement of coverage, it is important to recognise that smoking cessation violates some 'first principles' of what ought to be covered if this matter is considered from the traditional insurance perspective. True insurance has characteristics that are precisely opposed to those that apply to the treatment of nicotine addiction: it covers very high-cost events that have a very low probability of occurring and that are not affected by the existence of the insurance coverage. A classic example is homeowner's fire insurance. A home fire can be an extremely costly event; it occurs very rarely; and the probability of a fire is not increased by virtue of the homeowner's being insured (except in the rare instance of arson for profit).

In the case of the treatment of smoking, the cost is relatively low (a significant burden only to the truly medically indigent, who may be spending more on cigarettes than they would on treatment), the 'risk' is high – many smokers seek aid in quitting – and the probability of receiving therapy is clearly influenced by coverage of it. Indeed, a principal reason that so many health professionals advocate coverage of smoking-cessation treatment (and other preventive services) is precisely to increase its utilisation.[35]

Under such circumstances, coverage of smoking-cessation therapy is correctly viewed as a subsidy, rather than as 'insurance'. The question then becomes why healthcare payers should subsidise a relatively low-cost, discretionary event that primarily affects the insured. Some would argue that one person's smoking cessation produces benefits for the broader society, but this argument stretches the concept of positive externality.[36] Others support coverage because they do not believe that 'enough' people will receive treatment if they have to pay for it directly by themselves, and they 'should' receive it. Whatever else its merits may be, this argument amounts to paternalism, pure and simple. Still others might emphasise the economic burden that treatment will impose on the poor; but at most, this recommends covering treatment for the genuinely poor, not for everyone.

As noted above, coverage seems warranted primarily for another reason: much of the current system of coverage in the US, and in many other countries, subsidises a variety of services that are inexpensive and discretionary, while also covering the truly insurable event, such as unpredictable and financially catastrophic serious illnesses. In this context, for smoking cessation (and other cost-effective preventive services[37]) to compete on a level playing field, smoking-cessation treatment ought to be covered as well. Given the impressive cost effectiveness of smoking cessation, it should be encouraged in an environment in which its absence will often result in much larger healthcare expenditures at a later date.[20]

If these are the philosophical arguments favouring or opposing coverage of smoking-cessation treatment, there are some practical barriers to achieving widespread coverage in a financing environment such as that characterising the US. Providers in the US are struggling to keep costs down (as, of course, are financing agencies in many countries). Their concerns are not simply whether procedures are cost effective, but whether they are cost saving. Their perception is that covering smoking cessation, or any of a number of other preventive services that are not currently covered, will increase costs, forcing them to increase premiums charged to their members.[38] In particular, if the environment is competitive, as it is in the US, providers will be reluctant to add to their costs in the absence of a demonstrably strong demand for the additional coverage, demand that will not wither in the face of rising premiums.

Evidence indicates that smoking cessation eventually pays for itself through reductions in later healthcare costs[20] (for example, related to a decreased incidence of lung cancer and heart disease). However, while reductions in later costs may more than cover the intervention costs for the society as a whole, individual providers are at risk of incurring the expense without realising the benefits. In fact, they even face the prospect that their competitors will realise the benefits, as individuals who quit smoking under their plan move, a few years later, to a competitors' plan.

The economic incentives may be correct at the societal level, but, in a country like the US, not necessarily at the level of the individual decision-maker. As such, if widespread coverage is to be achieved, it may have to be mandated by the responsible government agencies. Ironically, the economic incentive to cover smoking may increase in the US in the future, as providers continue to consolidate within catchment areas, thereby gaining monopoly control within the region. With fewer competitors and hence lower turnover rates, providers may realistically anticipate capturing more of the long term benefits of their investments in smoking cessation.

A similar problem plagues the creation of demand for coverage, which lies at the core of securing coverage in a nonmandated environment: both providers and patients remain to be convinced that treatment of nicotine addiction is very efficacious. For both parties, even the most effective treatments fail more often, usually 3, 4 or 5 times more often, than they succeed. The cost effectiveness of smoking-cessation interventions reflects their very low cost relative to their modest success rates, and the health-related importance of success. Thus, although society as a whole would benefit enormously from widespread application of treatment techniques, individual practitioners and smokers may remain sceptical. Financing agencies, worried about increased costs, will find a low-demand service easy to ignore.

However, in the absence of mandates to cover smoking cessation (and other cost-effective prevention services), the increasing use of performance 'report cards' may hasten the demand for coverage. In the US, the National Committee on Quality Assurance has included tobacco-intervention performance measures in its Health Plan Employer and Data Information Set (HEDIS) 3.0 'report card', and a similar performance evaluation by the Foundation for Accountability also creates incentives for providers to 'score well' on the delivery of prevention services. This information creation and diffusion process augurs a brighter future for the inclusion of smoking cessation and other preventive measures in providers' covered services.

The US government agency charged with developing clinical practice guidelines on the basis of effectiveness and cost effectiveness has recently recommended that NRT be offered to all smokers who are seeking assistance in quitting.[1] Ironically, as the various forces move providers toward covering the costs of preventive services, the availability of OTC NRT products may reduce provider interest in supporting smoking-cessation treatment within the healthcare setting. Physicians may be instructed to encourage smoking patients to buy NRT products over the counter, possibly with a prescription benefit, but physician counselling may remain no better than it is today.

## 4. Discussion

A cursory review such as this cannot hope to do justice to the myriad of often complicated issues that pervade the interpretation of a body of analytic literature. For example, the fact that differing methods of analysis, as well as measures of variables of interest, complicate comparison of the bottom-line findings of studies has been mentioned only in passing. If study A had employed the methods and measures used in study B, the cost-effectiveness findings in study A would undoubtedly have differed quantitatively, if not necessarily qualitatively. Readers wishing to know more about the commonly practised methods of CEA, as well as areas of controversy, should consult other publications on this class of analytical techniques.[15,25,39-41] Many such publications have primarily focused on pharmaceutical applications.[22-24]

Even many of the leading publications give short shrift to profoundly important (if seemingly intractable) problems, such as how to represent what are perhaps the most important costs (and benefits) in behaviour-changing interventions: those related to the psychosocial consequences of the behaviour, or of changes to it, for the individual receiving the therapy. In contemplating the smoking-cessation CEA literature, it is sobering to recognise that the principal outcomes – whether or not an individual participates in a treatment, and whether or not a participant succeeds in quitting – rest primarily on variables that are physiological and psychosocial in nature, including the physical and psychological reactions to addiction, social dependence and withdrawal.

These critical variables are never quantified explicitly in the CEAs. Were they reducible to numbers, they almost certainly would dominate those costs and benefits that comprise today's behaviour-change CEAs. It is interesting to consider, however, that at least some such factors do find their way into the existing studies, albeit indirectly and essentially invisibly. For example, the ability of NRT to ease the problems associated with nicotine withdrawal clearly contributes to the enhanced effectiveness of therapies that include NRT. In essence, NRT reduces a physiological and psychosocial cost that limits the effectiveness of other interventions, although it is never quantified as a financial cost in CEAs of those interventions. Were it included, it is possible that the lower cost-effectiveness ratios found for the 'low-tech' interventions would lose some of their relative attractiveness; the gap between the 'real' cost-effectiveness ratios of the 'low-tech' and the NRT-based 'high-tech' interventions might be substantially smaller than the gap between reported ratios.

Does the failure to incorporate these important costs and benefits into contemporary CEAs invalidate the findings of the literature, or substantially diminish their importance? Not for the purposes contemplated here. Although the omission of psychosocial considerations plagues behaviour-change intervention research in particular, the same problem is present in virtually all matters pertaining to health and healthcare. Regardless, resource-allocation decisions must be made, and the consumption of measurable resources, compared with the health benefits derived, is a legitimate and fundamental concern in striving to improve healthcare-resource allocation. Inclusion of psychosocial costs and benefits in the CEA calculation, were it possible, would help us to predict successful smoking cessation, but it would not address the consumption of tangible, scarce resources any better than do the existing published studies.

## 5. Conclusion

Despite its flaws, the CEA literature constitutes a good guide to efficient utilisation of resources, and to the making of financing decisions therefrom. The smoking-cessation CEAs are particularly useful in this regard, because of the consistency of their findings of substantial benefits to health for modest investments. However, translating study findings into healthcare policy represents yet another challenge.

## Acknowledgements

Preparation of this paper was assisted by a grant from the Robert Wood Johnson Foundation, Princeton, NJ. I am indebted to two anonymous reviewers for helpful comments.

## References

1.  Fiore MC, Bailey WC, Cohen SJ, et al. Smoking cessation. Clinical Practice Guideline no. 18. US Department of Health and Human Services, Public Health Service. AHCPR Publication No. 96-0692. Rockville (MD): Agency for Health Care Policy and Research, Apr 1996
2.  Slama K, Karsenty S, Hirsch A. Effectiveness of minimal intervention by general practitioners with their smoking patients: a randomised, controlled trial in France. Tobacco Control 1995; 4: 162-9
3.  Oster G, Huse DM, Delea TE, et al. Cost-effectiveness of nicotine gum as an adjunct to physician's advice against cigarette smoking. JAMA 1986; 256: 1315-8
4.  Fiscella K, Franks P. Cost-effectiveness of the transdermal nicotine patch as an adjunct to physicians' smoking cessation counseling. JAMA 1996; 275: 1247-51
5.  Eddy DM. David Eddy ranks the tests. Harvard Health Letter 1992; Jul Suppl.: 10-11
6.  Altman DG, Flora JA, Fortmann SP, et al. The cost-effectiveness of three smoking cessation programs. Am J Public Health 1987; 77: 162-5
7.  Windsor RA, Warner KE, Cutter GR. A cost-effectiveness analysis of self-help smoking cessation methods for pregnant women. Public Health Rep 1988; 103: 83-8
8.  Tillgren P, Rosen M, Haglund BJ, et al. Cost-effectiveness of a tobacco 'quit and win' contest in Sweden. Health Policy 1993; 26: 43-53
9.  Tillgren P, Haglund BJ, Ainetdin T, et al. Effects of different intervention strategies in the implementation of a nationwide tobacco 'quit and win' contest in Sweden. Tobacco Control 1995; 4: 344-50
10. Cummings SR, Rubin SM, Oster G. The cost-effectiveness of counseling smokers to quit. JAMA 1989; 261: 75-9
11. Ershoff DH, Quinn VP, Mullen PD, et al. Pregnancy and medical cost outcomes of a self-help prenatal smoking cessation program in an HMO. Public Health Rep 1990; 105: 340-7
12. Marks JS, Koplan JP, Hogue CJ, et al. A cost-benefit/cost-effectiveness analysis of smoking cessation for pregnant women. Am J Prev Med 1990; 6: 282-9
13. Windsor RA, Lowe JB, Perkins LL, et al. Health education for pregnant smokers: its behavioral impact and cost benefit. Am J Public Health 1993; 83: 201-6
14. Hueston WJ, Mainous AG III, Farrell JB. A cost-benefit analysis of smoking cessation programs during the first trimester of pregnancy for the prevention of low birthweight. J Fam Pract 1994; 39: 353-7
15. Warner KE, Luce BR. Cost-benefit and cost-effectiveness analysis in health care: principles, practice, and potential. Ann Arbor (MI): Health Administration Press, 1982
16. Hodgson TA. Cigarette smoking and lifetime medical expenditures. Milbank Q 1992; 70: 81-125
17. Wagner EH, Curry SJ, Grothaus L, et al. The impact of smoking and quitting on health care use. Arch Intern Med 1995; 155: 1789-95
18. Krumholz HM, Cohen BJ, Tsevat J, et al. Cost-effectiveness of a smoking cessation program after myocardial infarction. J Am Coll Cardiol 1993; 22: 1697-702
19. McGhan WF Smith MD. Pharmacoeconomic analysis of smoking-cessation interventions. Am J Health Syst Pharm 1996; 53: 45-52
20. Warner KE, Smith RJ, Smith DG, Fries BE. Health and economic implications of a work-site smoking cessation program: a simulation analysis. J Occup Environ Med 1996; 38: 981-92
21. Elixhauser A. The costs of smoking and the cost effectiveness of smoking-cessation programs. J Public Health Policy 1990; 11: 218-37
22. Luce BR. Cost-effectiveness analysis: obstacles to standardisation and its use in regulating pharmaceuticals. Pharmacoeconomics 1993; 3: 1-9
23. Drummond MF. Cost-effectiveness guidelines for reimbursement of pharmaceuticals: is economic evaluation ready for its enhanced status? Health Econ 1992; 1: 85-92
24. Drummond MF. Economic evaluation of pharmaceuticals: science or marketing? Pharmacoeconomics 1992; 2: 8-13
25. Gold MR, Siegel JE, Russell LB, et al. Cost-effectiveness in health and medicine. New York: Oxford University Press, 1996
26. Tengs TO, Adams ME, Pliskin JS, et al. Five-hundred life-saving interventions and their cost-effectiveness. Risk Anal 1995; 15: 369-90